BackUp TRAX

Basic Blues For Guitar

by Dix Bruce

Online Audio www.melbay.com/97224BCDEB

Audio Contents:

1. Introduction
2. & 3. Tuning
4. Memphis Minnie Blues *(slow)*
5. Memphis Minnie Blues *(excerpt)*
6. Memphis Minnie Blues *(with band)*
7. Born to Die *(slow)*
8. Born to Die *(excerpt)*
9. Born to Die *(with band)*
10. When I Lay My Burden Down *(slow)*
11. When I Lay My Burden Down *(excerpt)*
12. When I Lay My Burden Down *(with band)*
13. Kissin' Ain't No Crime *(slow)*
14. Kissin' Ain't No Crime *(excerpt)*
15. Kissin' Ain't No Crime *(with band)*
16. T-Model Ford Blues *(slow)*
17. T-Model Ford Blues *(excerpt)*
18. T-Model Ford Blues *(with band)*
19. Cm Blues *(slow)*
20. Cm Blues *(excerpt)*
21. Cm Blues *(with band)*
22. Honey Babe *(slow)*
23. Honey Babe *(excerpt)*
24. Honey Babe *(with band)*
25. The Highway Blues *(slow)*
26. The Highway Blues *(excerpt)*
27. The Highway Blues *(with band)*
28. Jump Blues *(slow)*
29. Jump Blues *(excerpt)*
30. Jump Blues *(with band)*
31. Frogs For Snakes *(slow)*
32. Frogs For Snakes *(excerpt)*
33. Frogs For Snakes *(with band)*
34. Gm Blues *(slow)*
35. Gm Blues *(excerpt)*
36. Gm Blues *(with band)*
37. Tuxedo Blues *(slow)*
38. Tuxedo Blues *(excerpt)*
39. Tuxedo Blues *(with band)*
40. Rockabilly Boogie *(slow)*
41. Rockabilly Boogie *(excerpt)*
42. Rockabilly Boogie *(with band)*
43. Cream in My Coffee *(slow)*
44. Cream in My Coffee *(excerpt)*
45. Cream in My Coffee *(with band)*

Cover photo by Dix Bruce. Guitar courtesy of R.E. Phillips Metal Guitars, Martinez, Ca.

Audio recording produced by Dix Bruce, Audio recorded by Jim Nunally & Dix Bruce.

MEL BAY

I0806902

2 3 4 5 6 7 8 9 0

Book and Audio Play-along Set!
Includes melodies, chord diagrams and guitar tablature.

Let us be YOUR band! We'll Jam All Night Long!

- **Play along with hot blues rhythm sections:** guitar, bass, drums, piano and harmonica. Turn it on, play along, and you've got the makings of a dynamite jam session! Work out on **Country and Urban Blues, Acoustic and Electric Blues, Delta Blues, Texas Blues, Chicago Blues, Slide Guitar Blues, Traditional and Modern Blues** in many different major and minor keys.
- **You play all the leads**—the band backs you up. Learn melodies and practice soloing on 14 great blues in a variety of styles, tempos and keys.
- **Learn the best way, the fun way—*by doing.*** Repeat a tune or passage as many times as you wish. We never get tired and *WE'LL JAM ALL NIGHT LONG!*
- **Beginners & Intermediate** players can practice basic skills. **Advanced** players can hone their improvisation chops.
- **Everyone learns at his or her own individual pace.**
- **Melodies** are first presented on the recording at a slow speed with just guitar, then repeated at regular speed with the band. Finally, the band plays several choruses and you play all the leads.
- **Repeat songs,** at slow or regular speed, as many times as you wish, perfect phrases, melodies and solos in a band context.

Potential for improvement is unlimited.

The band never gets tired. We'll jam all night long!

Comments on BackUp TRAX:

"...Superb, a must for every student's library...Allows the student to learn with a professional rhythm section, experiment with as many soloing ideas as he or she can muster, and most importantly, to develop the art of improvisation while enjoying every moment of his or her practice session. I wholeheartedly recommend this to all of my students..."

—(Elvo D'Amante: Music educator, Laney College, Oakland, CA.)

"What a fantastic job. The recording allows me to play while repeating, stopping, getting lost — no live band or teacher would put up with that. If players could hear your tape just once, you'd sell a million copies!"

—(J. R. - Pensacola, FL)

"...beautifully packaged, equally valuable for both aspiring and experienced jazz musicians."

—(Floyd Levin - Jersey Jazz)

Table of Contents

How BackUp TRAX Work:

Here's how **BackUp TRAX** work: You play along with the recording,read the music, and learn melodies and solos to some of the most popular tunes in the **Blues, Traditional Jazz/Dixieland, Early Jazz & Hot Tunes, Old Time and Fiddle Tunes, or Swing & Jazz** repertoire.Then practice improvising and soloing!

- **First** you'll hear a tune's melody, with just guitar backup, at a speed slow enough for beginners.
- **Next** you'll hear the melody once again, this time with the whole band, at regular speed.
- **After that,** the band plays several choruses of the tune and you supply the melody or solo! Split-track stereo recording allows you to hear just lead, just rhythm, or both, so you can isolate parts for specific study. Repeat a song, at either speed, as many times as you wish, perfecting phrases, melodies and solos in a band context without tiring your back up musicians. Beginners can practice basic skills while more advanced players can hone their improvisation chops, each at his or her own individual learning rate. Potential for improvement is unlimited. You'll be amazed at your progress when you regularly jam with BackUp TRAX. It's just like playing with a band, and you're the star soloist.

Let us be YOUR band, we'll jam all night long!

Dix Bruce is a musician and writer from the San Francisco Bay Area. He has produced over thirty five music instruction books, audio recordings, and videos for Mel Bay Publications. He performs and records with several groups in the San Francisco Bay Area including a guitar duo with Jim Nunally (see CD info below) and The Royal Society Jazz Orchestra, a ten-piece big band which performs jazz from the 1920s and 1930s. He has been a frequent contributor to FRETS, Fretted Instrument Guild of America magazine, Acoustic Guitar, Flatpicking Guitar, Acoustic Musician, and other publications.

ALSO By Dix Bruce:

BackUp TRAX: Old Time & Fiddle Tunes Vol. I. Book/Audio set (Mel Bay).
BackUp TRAX: Swing & Jazz Vol. I. Book/Audio set (Mel Bay).
BackUp Trax: Old Time & Fiddle Tunes for Cello. Book/Audio set (Mel Bay).
Basic Swing Guitar. DVD (Guitar Workshop).
Basic Country Flatpicking Guitar. DVD (Guitar Workshop).
Famous Mandolin Pickin' Tunes. Book/Audio set (Mel Bay).
First Lessons® Mandolin. Book/Audio/Video set (Mel Bay).
Getting Into® Bluegrass Mandolin. Book/Audio set (Mel Bay).
Guide to Capo, Transposing & The Nashville Numbering System. Book (Mel Bay).
Parking Lot Picker's Songbook: Banjo Edition by Dix Bruce & Bill Evans. Book/Audio set (Mel Bay).
Parking Lot Picker's Songbook: Guitar Edition. Book/Audio set (Mel Bay).
Parking Lot Picker's Songbook: Mandolin Edition. Book/Audio set (Mel Bay).
Shady Grove: Acoustic Guitar Solos. Book (Mel Bay).
String Band Classics: Mandolin. Book/Audio set (Mel Bay).
String Band Classics: Guitar. Book/Audio set (Mel Bay).
You Can Teach Yourself® Country Guitar. Book/Audio/Video set (Mel Bay).
You Can Teach Yourself® Mandolin. Book/Audio/Video set (Mel Bay).
Brothers at Heart. CD by Dix Bruce & Jim Nunally.
From Fathers to Sons. CD by Dix Bruce & Jim Nunally. A collection of traditional American vocal and instrumental music learned from the duo's musical parents and played on two acoustic guitars.
In My Beautiful Dream. CD by Dix Bruce & Jim Nunally.
The Way Things Are. CD by Dix Bruce & Jim Nunally. Mostly original songs by Dix & Jim plus classics by some of America's greatest songwriters.
My Folk Heart. CD by Dix Bruce. Solo & small group traditional American folk music (Musix C-101).
Tuxedo Blues. CD by Dix Bruce. String swing & jazz and new acoustic string music (Musix C-102). Includes "Tuxedo Blues" and a version of "Cream in My Coffee" from this book.

Available at better music stores or direct from **MUSIX**, PO Box 231005, Pleasant Hill, CA 94523.
Musix website: **www.musixnow.com**

Foreword to **BackUp TRAX**

When I was first learning to play leads on the guitar, an older and wiser musician friend suggested that I practice with taped rhythm sections. The idea was to record myself on rhythm guitar, then listen to the track and play along. That way I could hear the chords, practice playing over them in the context of the song's form, and repeat whatever I was working on until I'd perfected it. It was almost as good as playing with a live band and offered the opportunity of infinite repetition as I honed this lick or that solo, all without wearing out my musical welcome with my friends! For the past twenty years I have included rhythm track playing in my daily practice routine.

To say that it helped me enormously would be an understatement. My melodies and solos got better—cleaner, and more focused. As I practiced solos or licks hundreds of times, my timing and rhythm playing improved. I owe a great deal of my playing ability to this type of practice.

Because of my positive experiences with practice tapes, I decided to round up some of the best musicians in the San Francisco Bay Area, capture grooves to the most popular tunes and progressions of different genres on tape, and let you play along. **BackUp TRAX** are the result. **BackUp TRAX** give musicians a rhythm section to play along with and rehearse melodies, solos, licks and rhythm playing. **BackUp TRAX** offers the advantage of infinite repetition; you can work on a tune, solo or passage for hours, perfecting it without wearing out your fellow players. Opportunities for advancing your reading and improvising skills while expanding your repertoire are unlimited.

Each **BackUp TRAX** set comes with a book of melodies, chord charts, playing tips and an audio recording to listen to and play along with. Melodies to each of the tunes are recorded at about one half speed with just piano or guitar accompaniment so you can study the tune at a slow tempo before playing it at regular speed with the full band. This is followed by a regular speed, full-band version of the same tune where you supply all of the leads. Instruments are isolated and panned to the right or left stereo channel for maximum flexibility. By adjusting the balance control on your stereo amplifier you can hear: 1) the full band with melodies; 2) basic rhythm with melodies; or 3) just basic rhythm. Tones for tuning are at the beginning of each recording. Turn it on, play along, and you've got the makings of dynamite jam session. You learn the best way, the fun way, by doing. And, we'll jam all night long!

So, have fun, good luck and happy playing!

—Dix Bruce

Photo by Rob Thomas

Dix Bruce

Introduction to **BackUp TRAX: Basic Blues**

Welcome to **BackUp TRAX: Basic Blues** — fourteen pieces carefully chosen to represent a variety of tunes and keys encountered in the basic blues repertoire. **BackUp TRAX: Basic Blues** is a sampler of Country and Urban Blues, Acoustic and Electric Blues, Delta Blues, Texas Blues, Chicago Blues, Slide Guitar Blues, Traditional and Modern Blues in many different major and minor keys. Each tune is played by a crack backup band: guitar, bass, drums, keyboards and harmonica, which is sure to inspire you to play your best.

Each tune is presented at the slow speed first, followed by the regular speed version with melody, and finally, the regular speed version where you supply all the leads. In each case the melody is panned to the right channel to allow you to isolate it as you study. The rhythm section is panned to the left channel (guitar on the slow versions, most of the band on the regular speed versions) so that you can also isolate it. Tuning tones are included at the beginning of the audio.

Tips for working with BackUp TRAX: Basic Blues

I designed **BackUp TRAX** to be a rhythm section for players of all abilities to jam along with and work out their soloing ideas. Though **BackUp TRAX** are not intended to be method books for improvising in the given style, I will offer suggestions here and there on how to approach the individual tunes. There are many good blues guitar methods on the market which examine the scales, chords and other elements that make up the style. The most important thing, though, is for you to play what you feel and discover your own voice in the process. This process is analogous to learning a new language: melodies, riffs, keys, and scales are your musical vocabulary, grammar and syntax. Along the way you'll experiment with different elements and discover how to combine them in ways that feel most natural to you and express your feelings best. The goal is to make the process second nature by training your head, fingers, and soul in the mechanics of playing your instrument in your style. Ultimately it'll become as automatic as speech. Along the way, the most important thing is to have fun as you take the music wherever you want it to go.

Here are a few suggestions for working with **BackUP TRAX: Basic Blues.**

1) Before you play, familiarize yourself with the melodies and chord progressions of each tune by listening and reading along.

2) Once you're acquainted with the tunes, memorize the melodies while playing along with the slow version of the piece. Gradually work your way up to the regular speed version. *Knowing a song's melody and chord progression is essential in the improvisation process.* Older blues and jazz players I know refer to improvisation as "takeoff," where the melody is the starting point for elaborating or "taking off" from the tune and inventing new melodic ideas.

3) Analyze the chords. All of the tunes are written with the classic chord progressions and in the various styles of basic blues. You'll find that the blues repertoire, literally thousands of tunes, is largely based on a very few distinct chord progressions combined in different ways to make up most of the tunes. Because of this simplicity of form, the blues genre is universal the world over.

Recognizing these progressions is essential to understanding how a tune works and how it relates to other similar tunes. Note the number of measures in the form, for example, twelve bar blues, sixteen bar blues, or twenty four bar blues. Identify the key a tune is in and whether it's major or minor. Learn to recognize the elements of the progression and which chords are played where. For example, "two measures of **I** (one) followed by two measures of **IV** (four)." It's especially important to identify the chords by their Roman numeral names, which define a chord's function in a progression and key as opposed to their letter names which reveal much less. You'll also find that most professional musicians refer to chords in keys by their Roman numerals. It's a clear and concise way to communicate on stage and makes transposing from one key to another much easier.

It all begins with the major scale. Look at the C major scale below with its notes (also called "scale degrees") numbered. Notice that we use Arabic and *not* Roman numerals. Generally Arabic numerals are used to name notes in a scale, Roman numerals to name chords in a key. "Wh" and "1/2" identify the whole and half step intervals between the notes of the major scale. Each major scale has seven different notes, "do" to "ti," and seven different chords built on and named by them. This will remain the same for every key.

	C	D	E	F	G	A	B	C
Scale #	**1**	**2**	**3**	**4**	**5**	**6**	**7**	**8**
	do	**re**	**mi**	**fa**	**sol**	**la**	**ti**	**do**

wh   wh   1/2   wh   wh   wh   1/2

If we use only the notes from the C major scale and build three note or "triad" chords on each of these scale notes here's what we get:

(Key of C)	**C**	**Dm**	**Em**	**F**	**G**	**Am**	**B°**
	I	**ii**	**iii**	**IV**	**V**	**vi**	**vii**

m = minor, ° = diminished

In the above example, the chords are made up using only the notes of the C major scale. Blues, pop and jazz composers often change these minor chords, like those above, to dominant seven chords for melodic and creative interest. These chords can appear as minor or major, and the term "one-six-two-five" can apply to either. "Highway Blues" (page 33) has a "one-six-two-five" chord progression.

My friend, Professor Elvo D'Amante, author of the book "All About Chords" (Encore Music, PO Box 315, Orinda, CA 94563), gets quite annoyed when I call the D7 in the key of C a "two chord." He recommends referring to the D7 in the key of C as the "five of five." The reasoning is that the D7 is functioning as a dominant chord in the key of G where it's the five chord and for those few measures, the song feels like the key of G. He further suggests that the best way to refer to the A7 chord in the key of C is as the "five of two," again reasoning that the A7, a dominant chord, is functioning as the five chord in the key of D. Whether correct, incorrect or annoying, musicians on gigs usually use the "one-six-two-five" lexicon to communicate progressions to one another on stage. Sometimes you'll have to determine whether a chord is minor or dominant by its context, as you hear the tune the first time through. This can be exciting, especially in front of an audience! Of course I-VI-II-V (VI, II and V dominant chords) is very different from I-vi-ii-V (vi and ii minor chords) and the two are not interchangeable. But, melodies or riffs that fit over one I-vi-ii-V will work over any other I-vi-ii-V as with I-VI-II-V, provided they are used in the same key or transposed correctly.

Try not to be confused by different keys, chords or transposing. Look at the chord changes in the context of the tune's home key. The point is to study how the chords in any song fit together and recognize them numerically (I, ii, iii, IV, V, vi, vii) rather than alphabetically (G, Am, Bm, C, D, Em, F♯°). That way you'll see that a ii chord (Am) in the key of G functions exactly like a ii chord (B♭m) in the key of A♭ and a VI chord (A7) in the key of C functions exactly like a VI chord (B♭7) in the key of D♭. You can play the same melody, transposed by one half step, in each key, over chords with the same function.

From there you can compare similar tunes or similar parts of tunes to expand your understanding of a whole genre of music. This will help you build a "generic" approach to playing the repertoire. You can then look at any new tune as a combination of parts, for example, "ii-V-I" ("two - five - one") in G followed by ii-V-i ("two - five - one") in A minor, then a III-VI-II-V ("three - six - two - five") bridge. Understanding the individual parts will help you tackle the whole. Try to relate these tunes and progressions to other popular standards. Consult original sheet music or fake books for ideas. Look for overall similarities in progression and form and identify common chord passages that occur again and again. This will take some study, but you'll end up using these "chunks" as building blocks for understanding unfamiliar tunes and playing over their changes.

The chart on the next page illustrates many of these ideas. It shows the number of sharps or flats each key has in its key signature and the chords in each key along with their Roman numeral designations. It can be used as a scale chart by ignoring the chord designations. For example, in the key of A line we see: A Bm C♯m D E F♯m G♯°. If we ignore the minor ("m") and diminished ("°") designations, we're left with the A major scale: A B C♯ D E F♯ G♯.

The chart can also be used as a transposition chart. Find the horizontal line showing the key of the song you want to transpose. Identify which columns, I, ii, iii, IV, V, etc., the known notes or chords fall in. Then, simply read up or down to the new key and find the transposed chords. You can change the chords shown below from minors to majors and sevenths as your situation demands—just make sure your transposed chord has the same quality as the original. For example, let's use the C major row to transpose C, A7, D7, G7 from the key of C to the key of B♭. Change the chart's sixth chord Am to A7, follow down two rows to the key of Bf where we find Gm. Since our original chord from the key of C is an A7, this new chord should be a G7. So, the I-VI-II-V from the key of C becomes B♭-G7-C7-F7 in the key of B♭.

4) Everyone wants to be a great improviser. The dream is to be able to pick up your ax and just cook, making up chorus after chorus of brilliant material on the fly. On the way to doing that though, most of us hit the "Now What Do I Play?" wall. Here are a few general suggestions one can use to stimulate or restart the improvisation process.

Try learning each melody in another octave. Most of these melodies are reachable for most intermediate players, so you probably can move the melody up or down an octave. On many of the tunes guitar players can go both up and down an octave. If you can't reach every note, improvise! Maybe leave the note in question in its initial octave, or change it to something that you can reach. In the process you'll define your limits and probably stretch them.

Repetition is the engine of improvisation—after awhile, you'll get tired of playing something the same old way and gradually, often imperceptibly at first, begin changing it. These changes can be rhythmic or melodic, and they'll personalize your approach to a song.

Here are a couple of examples, the first from "Kissin' Ain't No Crime," (page 21); the second from "Memphis Minnie Blues," (page 13) where slight changes in the melody provide a good foundation for a more extensive improvisation.

Chord, Scale, & Transposition Chart

		Scale	***1***	***2***	***3***	***4***	***5***	***6***	***7***	***8 (1)***
Key	**♯ - ♭**	***Chord***	**I**	**ii**	**iii**	**IV**	**V**	**vi**	**vii**	**VIII (I)**
C	none		C	Dm	Em	F	G	Am	B°	C
F	1 - ♭		F	Gm	Am	B♭	C	Dm	E°	F
B♭	2 - ♭		B♭	Cm	Dm	E♭	F	Gm	A°	B♭
E♭	3 - ♭		E♭	Fm	Gm	A♭	B♭	Cm	D°	E♭
A♭	4 - ♭		A♭	B♭m	Cm	D♭	E♭	Fm	G°	A♭
D♭	5 - ♭		D♭	E♭m	Fm	G♭	A♭	B♭m	C°	D♭
G♭	6 - ♭		G♭	A♭m	B♭m	C♭	D♭	E♭m	F°	G♭
C♭	7 - ♭		C♭	D♭m	E♭m	F♭	G♭	A♭m	B♭°	C♭
C♯	7 - ♯		C♯	D♯m	E♯m	F♯	G♯	A♯m	B♯°	C♯
F♯	6 - ♯		F♯	G♯m	A♯m	B	C♯	D♯m	E♯°	F#
B	5 - ♯		B	C♯m	D♯m	E	F♯	G♯m	A♯°	B
E	4 - ♯		E	F♯m	G♯m	A	B	C♯m	D♯°	E
A	3 - ♯		A	Bm	C♯m	D	E	F♯m	G♯°	A
D	2 - ♯		D	Em	F♯m	G	A	Bm	C♯°	D
G	1 - ♯		G	Am	Bm	C	D	Em	F♯°	G

Kissing Ain't No Crime original melody:

Improvisation:

Chord diagrams for all the chords used in this book are shown in alphabetical order on page 47.

Memphis Minnie Blues original melody:

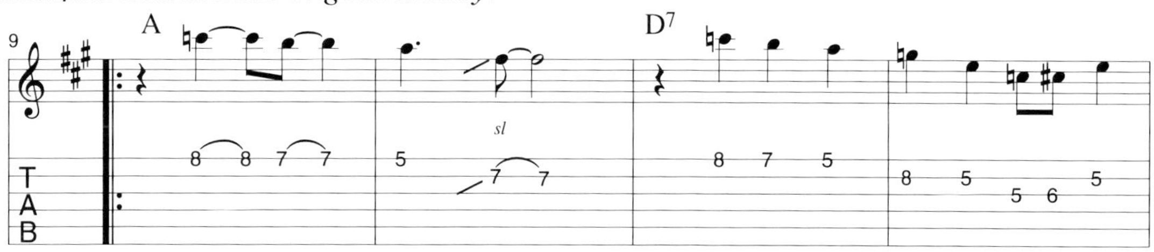

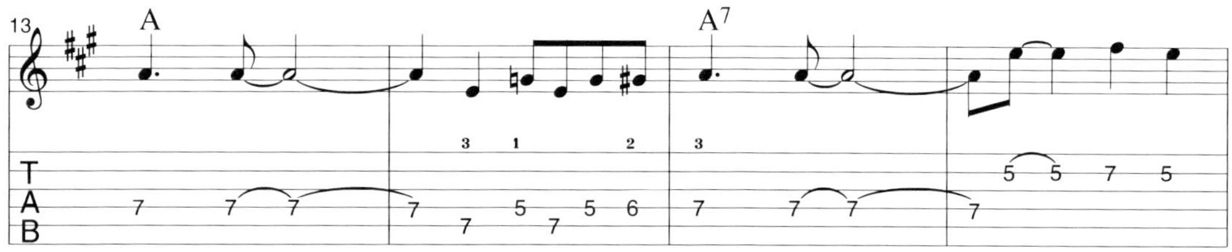

Improvisation:

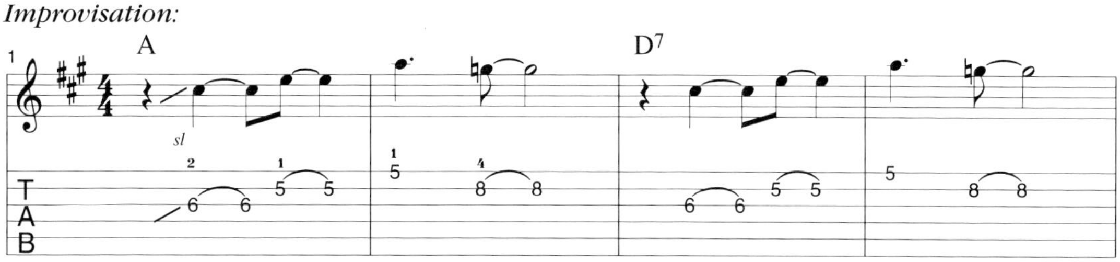

Over time you'll develop your own versions of these melodies until you have a composed solo. This process will be aided if you *study how other musicians play similar blues both live and on recordings. Don't limit yourself to musicians who play your instrument.* In fact you'll probably end up with more interesting results if you listen to different instrumentalists. It's not necessary to learn another player's riff or solo exactly—again, your playing will probably be more interesting in the long run if you work out your own version of what you hear.

Study how other musicians approach melodies and chord progressions. Try to incorporate their ideas into your playing. Isolate chunks of solos and analyze them according to the chords (I, VI, II, V, for example) they're played over. Keep track of your progress in a spiral bound music notebook as you either transcribe or invent melodic chunks or licks based on what you're hearing. (Notebooks are great for keeping all of your ideas in one place.) Then lift these licks from their given tunes and keys and play them over other tunes with the same chord progression. Transpose, modify, change and recycle them to include your own ideas. Make up your own licks. I've included suggested variations for most tunes which you can incorporate into your own ideas. Practice playing your solos and licks on other similar tunes and in other keys. All you have to do is look for matching chord changes, and plug them in, transposing when necessary. The slow versions of the tunes on the audio can help you create solos at a relaxed speed. To do all of this effectively requires a fair amount of discipline on your part but any effort will be rewarded with better technique and solos.

Most people who are learning to improvise want hard and fast rules about which notes to play. Unfortunately, (or fortunately!) music is much more abstract than that, and there are no real "rules" which, if applied, will automatically result in a wonderful solo. And I hesitate to offer rules or guidelines because the most interesting music is often made by breaking those rules! The point of all of this is to bring out the music that's inside of you, that comes from your experience. The trick to doing that is to break thorough all your limiting layers of ego, propriety, technique, music theory, etc., and get what's in your soul out to the world! How's that for a lofty goal? Probably easier said than done, and something you have to do for yourself on a spiritual rather than a physical or mechanical level.

However, on the mechanical side, on some of the tunes I'll suggest patterns, positions, or scales to try in your solos as a way of making you aware of some of the possible ways you can approach a tune. Use these to stimulate your own improvisation process and help you learn where different notes are on the fingerboard. While it's important to know note locations, try to avoid the temptation to run up and down the scales in your solos. Instead, strive to play a melody. The greatest players never think about scales or licks, just like you don't think about sentence structure or vocabulary as you speak. ("OK, now I'm gonna modify the verb and stress the definite object with the dangling participle and then tie it up in the predicate…")

Sing a melodic passage in your head before you play it. Practice by singing along with **BackUp TRAX.** Even if you think you can't sing, work out rhythmic and melodic ideas with your voice. You'll eventually use your knowledge of music and the guitar to say it through your instrument, but singing before you try to play can be a great help in internalizing the music you learn from scales, chords, riffs, etc. Throw your head back and shout it out!

The traditional rule of thumb for learning to play blues is to emphasize the "blue" notes of the scale as

G major scale

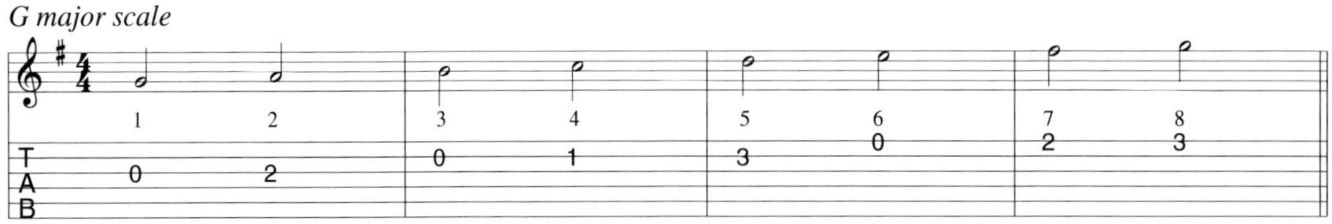

The natural third and seventh notes of the G major scale are B and F♯. To make them "blue" notes, we flat them (or lower them by 1/2 step) and the result is B♭ and F and the modified scale looks like this:

G major scale with flat 3 & 7

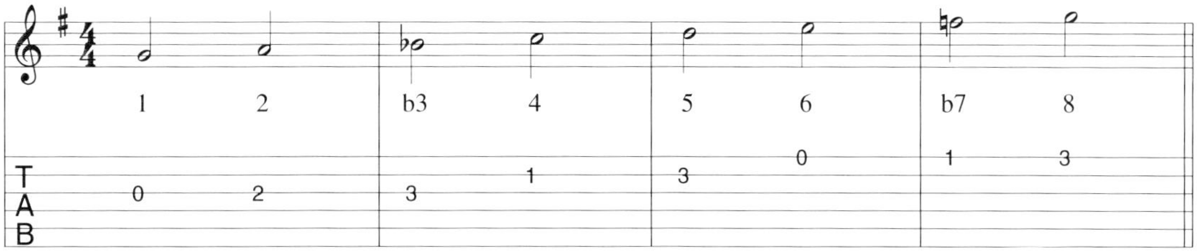

The quick and dirty way to apply this is to emphasize the flat 3 and flat 7 of the chord's scale you're playing over. In this case, we're playing over a G or G7 chord. If you're playing over a C or C7, flat the third and seventh of the C scale. You can go a step further and leave out a couple notes (the second and the sixth) to make the minor pentatonic scale. See the scale below.

G minor pentatonic

Again, use this over a G or G7 chord and change it accordingly for other chords and scales. Use these as building blocks to solos, not ends in and of themselves. They are not necessarily applicable to every type of chord or tune and there are millions of other approaches that may be more specific and better suited to a given situation or the way you play. Use them as a beginning and work from there. Think of scales as part of your musical alphabet. Strive to play a melody, not a scale! As you develop your musical ear, you'll find that you can flat other notes in the scale as well, not just the third and seventh.

5) Jamming. Great music is much more than just a rhythm section and a soloist. The ensemble playing is what makes or breaks a sound. Each player should listen to each of the others and shape the music collectively. Try to be conscious of supporting the other players when they solo. Help them play the best solo they can play. Kind of a musician's golden rule.

6) Don't forget to practice playing rhythm along with us. Make up your own rhythm riffs and work them. Start with the root of the chord and play a repeating rhythm riff with just that note. When the chord changes in the progression, change to the new root note but keep your basic rhythm riff. Work with the other notes of the chords as well as the complete chord. Put yourself into a supportive and rhythmic frame of mind. Give your fellow soloists what you like to hear when you're soloing. Your role here is to help them play their best just as theirs is to help you play your best. Don't fall into the "lead-itis" pit by ignoring your rhythmic role as part of the band. I once heard about a very mediocre guitarist who, when asked what style of guitar he played, answered, "I play LEAD guitar." Don't be that guy!

7) The tunes and their variations are presented in both standard notation and guitar tablature. The smaller numbers above the TAB staff indicate suggested fretting finger numbers. For right handed players, that's the left hand. For left handed players, it's the right. The letter designations on the TAB staff indicate suggested picking fingers (right for right handers, left for lefties) on the fingerpicked tunes:

T=thumb, i=index, m=middle, r=ring

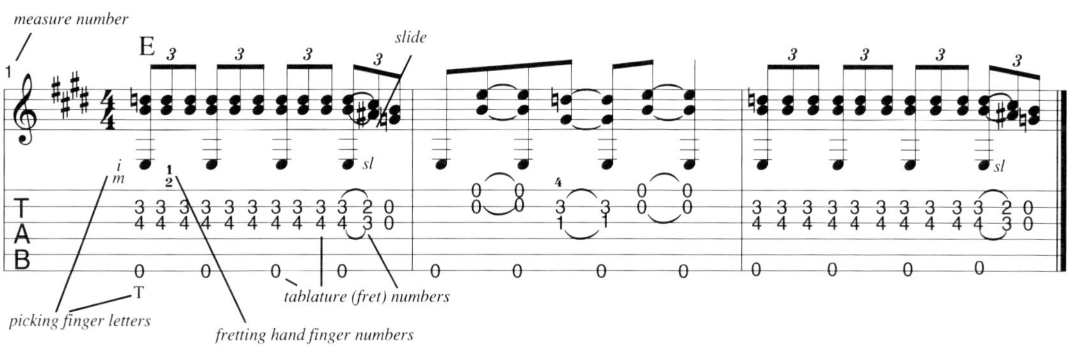

These position markers show how I play the notes and should be a starting place for you. Feel free to experiment and change them. In an effort to keep the music as uncluttered as possible, I added finger designations only where I felt they were absolutely necessary. Most of these designations will be obvious from the chord you are holding. In addition, the markers aren't repeated if a note or phrase recurs in the same position. In some of the fingerpicked tunes like "Frogs for Snakes," the music gets a little thick with TAB numbers, finger numbers, triplet numbers, and picking finger designations. In these cases, I moved the fretting finger numbers up near the standard notation. **Note:** if you're not a fingerpicker, you can still easily play any of the fingerpicked tunes. Simply leave out the thumb notes and play the upper note or notes with a flatpick.

The numbers to the left of the treble clef sign on each staff are measure numbers.

ho = hammer on, *sl* = slide, *po* = pull off.

8) The best general advice I can offer is to listen and play. Simple as that. It's very important that you hear what other players do, both live and on record, with these types of tunes and chord changes. Take the time to listen to your favorite recorded musicians play a lick or passage until you figure it out—a hundred times if necessary. Don't forget to sing what you're trying to play, even if you think you have a lousy voice. Look for new ideas and input constantly and try to make them a part of your playing. Most of all, remember that music is supposed to be fun, for both players and listeners. When it ain't fun, something's wrong! So, above all else, have fun! Now get in there and JAM!

Special thanks to the players on the recording: Chris Sandoval-drums; Steve Hanson-bass; Bruce Gordon-keyboards; Rick Hatfield-harmonica. That's me on guitar. Thanks also to Kathi Bruce, Annie Johnston, Bob Bergman, Charlotte Gibb and Jim Nunally for their incredibly helpful suggestions.

I'm always interested in hearing your comments, suggestions, and musician jokes. Write to me c/o **MUSIX**, PO Box 231005, Pleasant Hill, CA 94523. My website is: www.musixnow.com. My email address is: dix@musixnow.com

—Dix Bruce

Memphis Minnie Blues

Memphis Minnie was one of the greatest blues guitarists (excellent rhythm **and** lead), singers, and composers. She did it all with a great raw power and style during her heyday in the 1930s and 1940s. This tribute was inspired by her wonderful, funky rhythm guitar playing.

The tune, which I call an "uptempo country blues," begins with an introduction that's simply the last eight bars of the melody. These same eight bars are repeated after five choruses as an ending to the tune. "Memphis Minnie Blues," along with many others in this set, is known as a "riff blues." In these types of tunes, we take a simple two-, four-, or six-measure melodic phrase or "riff," play it over the first phrase of the form, repeat it over the second, and then play a different riff over the last phrase of the tune. In this case, each phrase is eight measures long.

The variation on the melody is based on turning the melodic shape upside down. Make it a habit to try doing the same thing with other melodies and licks. It can be a very effective tool for improvising on a melody. For example, if the original starts high and moves low, reverse it. For the second eight measures, we could repeat the first eight. Instead I moved the whole riff up five frets and played it out of the position suggested by the D7 chord in measure nine (M9). I did a similar thing with the E7 (M17) lick, simply moving it down two frets to play over the D7 chord (M19). This type of transposition is another technique of vital importance. Make it a point to learn riffs or whole melodies in closed positions and then move them up and down the fingerboard into new keys. The ability to transpose is invaluable!

"Memphis Minnie Blues," like any riff blues, can be made into something all your own relatively easily. All you need for a new solo is two new riffs. Fit the first riff over the first eight bars, repeat it over the second eight, plug in your other riff over the last eight. Make sure they fit with the chords. Practice with the slow version on the audio. Notice that the flat third (C natural) and the flat seven (G natural) of the A major scale figure prominently in the melody. Familiarize yourself with the notes I used in composing the melody by studying the tablature. The scale and scale position shown below should help. The small num-bers above the TAB numbers indicate suggested fret-ting fingers.

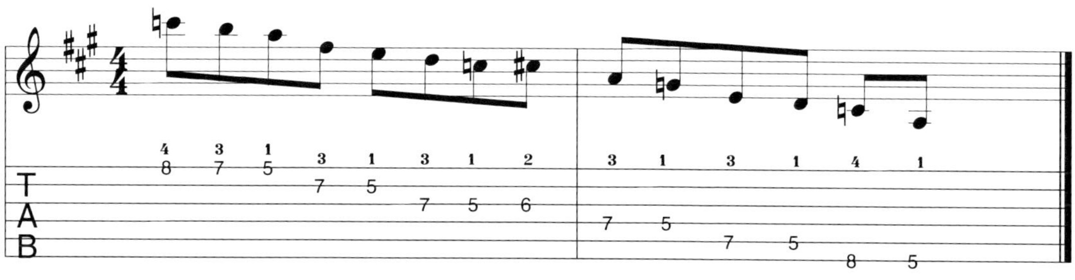

In general, blues chord progressions are predictable and we'll cover most of them in course of this book. Most begin and end on the same chord, usually the **I** chord. If the tune is repeated as you play additional choruses, a **V** chord is often added as a "turnaround" to bring the progression back to the I and the top of the form. (See the last two measures of "Memphis Minnie Blues" below.) However, the **last** time the progression is played, when the tune ends, the **V** is either omitted altogether or played for only a beat or two in favor of a strong **I**. Likewise, you'd probably change the last E notes in the melody to end on an A note.

24 measure form. Eight measure introduction, five choruses, eight measure ending. Key of A.

Memphis Minnie Blues

by Dix Bruce

After five choruses, repeat first eight bars as ending
Play A for last chord.

Memphis Minnie Blues variation

Born to Die

I used a glass bottleneck slide and an open D tuning to play the melody to this slow, lowdown, fingerpicked blues. Standard guitar tuning, highest pitched to lowest, is:

1	2	3	4	5	6
E	B	G	D	A	E

Lower strings 1, 2, 3, and 6 for the open D tuning:

1	2	3	4	5	6
D	A	F♯	D	A	D

In this basic type of fingerpicking, the bass notes, kind of a thumping drone on the root of the chord, are played with the thumb and the melody notes with the index finger in a pinching motion. I wear the slide on the pinkie finger of my left hand and use it to "fret" most of the notes, as you hear on the recording, I sometimes use my other left hand fingers to fret some of the notes, particularly those on the second and third strings. Note to flatpickers: you can play the melody with a flatpick, just leave out the bass notes.

For the rhythm guitar accompaniment, I played with a flatpick but muted the notes with the heel of my right hand as I picked to give a percussive sound. The ending is a four measure turnaround: one measure of the V chord (A7), one measure of the IV chord (G) and two measure of the I (D).

Spend a fair amount of time getting used to using a slide instead of fretting fingers. Practice on both chords and single strings. Since the guitar is tuned to an open D chord for this tune, simply laying a fretting finger or the slide over all the strings will give you a new chord at each fret. Play the open strings with no slide to get a D chord. Put it over the first fret wire for a D♯ or E♭ chord. Second fret gives you an E chord, and so on. Your chord will be most in tune if you place the slide directly over the fret wire, perpendicular to the neck, not in the space between fret wires as you are used to doing with your fingers. Of course you can get very interesting effects by sliding into the chord from above or below. You can also move the slide back and forth for a vibrato effect. Practice changing chords by playing along with other tunes on this audio, your favorite blues CDs, or in jams with other people. Start with simple two- and three- chord tunes and practice strumming the changes. Don't limit yourself to tunes in the key of D, since you can make any major chords with this tuning.

To play bluesy single notes, center the slide in the fret space between the fret wires and slide up or down to the notes. Moving the slide up and down just slightly will affect your tuning. It works much the same way as stretching strings to different pitches, another technique widely used in blues guitar.

Use the D minor pentatonic scale shown to familiarize yourself with the locations of the different notes along the first string, where most of the melody notes to "Born to Die" lie.

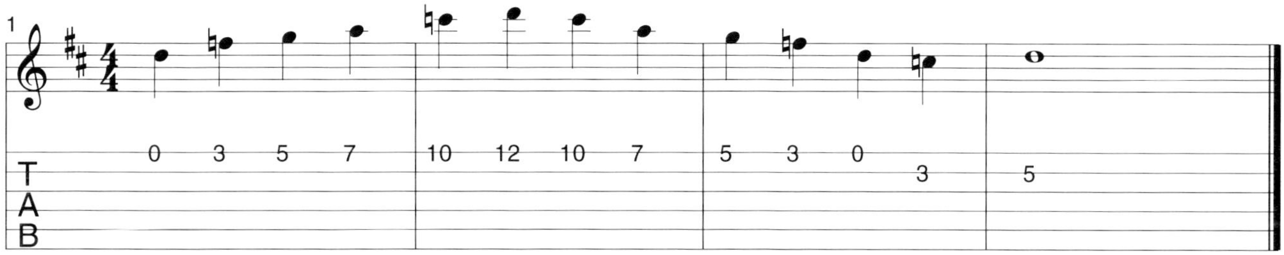

12 measure form. Three choruses, four measure turnaround ending. Key of D.

Born to Die

by Dix Bruce

Open D tuning:
D A F# D A D highest to lowest

When I Lay My Burden Down

When I Lay My Burden Down is a traditional "gospel/country blues" that is performed in blues and country contexts as well as traditional jazz and Dixieland. I asked bassist Steve Hanson to bow the bass like bassists in many of the early blues and string bands did. It gives the backup almost a jug band feel. Here, as on "Born to Die," the melody is fingerpicked, but again, you can play the melody with single string notes if you ignore the bass notes. The variation shown is a harmony to the melody. Try playing it with a friend.

16 measure form. Six choruses. Key of C Traditional

When I Lay My Burden Down harmony

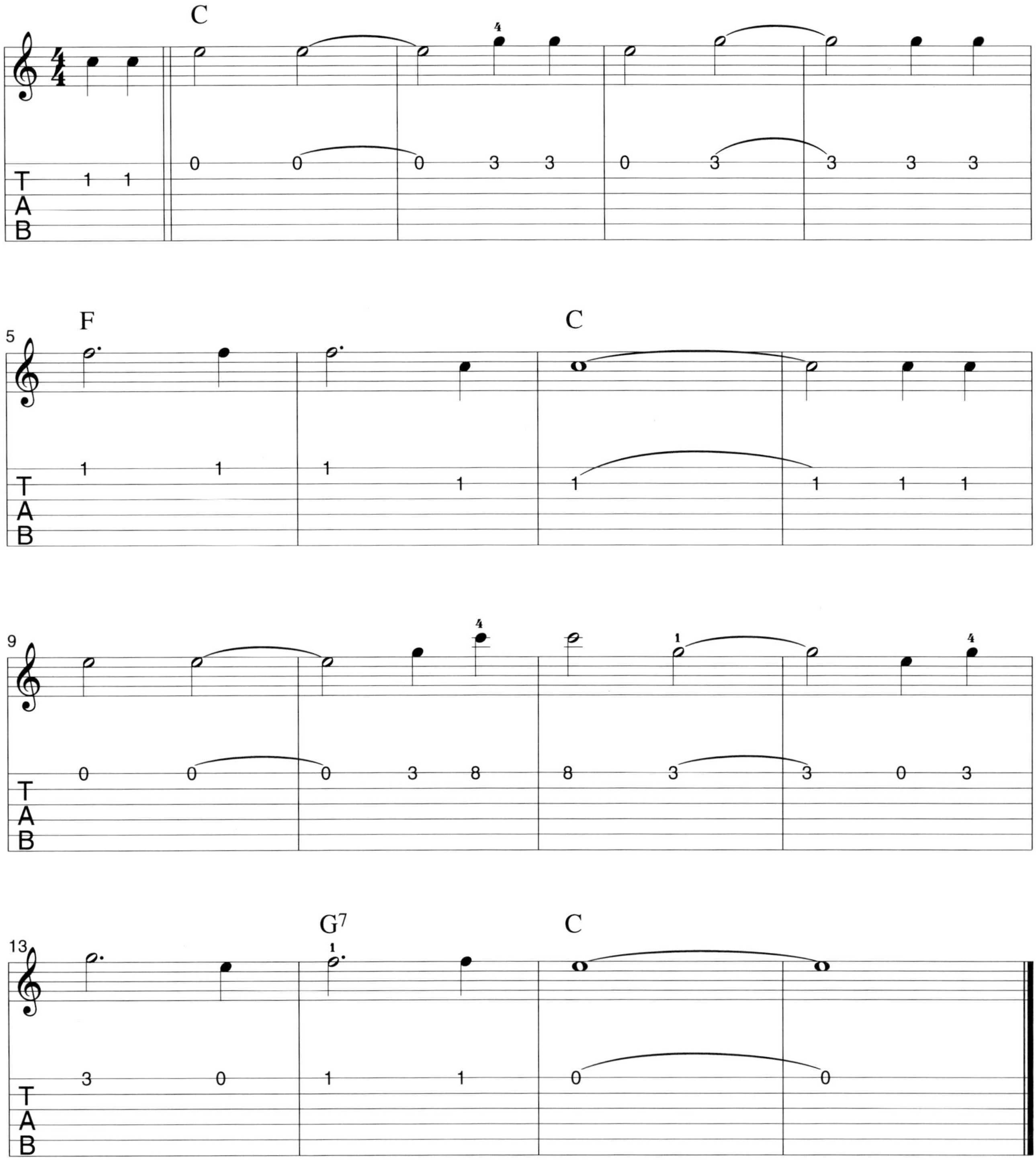

Kissin' Ain't No Crime

Kissin' Ain't No Crime is a 1950s Rhythm & Blues or New Orleans novelty-style song. Part of both the melody and the backup guitar riff are played with notes muted with the heel of the picking hand. The progression is a little different from straight blues and has a "verse, chorus" structure. The verse is a full eight bars of the I (C) chord before we get to any chord changes. Here's a chance to really work out on one chord.

The muted tone on both the melody and chord backup is accomplished by damping the strings with the heel of the picking hand. It's a bit of a trick to get just the right amount of pick attack with the right amount of muting so that the sound of the note can be heard along with the funkiness of the muting. Muted and unmuted sections are labeled in the music.

Experiment with flatting the third and the seventh of the C scale as well as using the C minor pentatonic scale. *(See below.)* Be sure to play them ascending and descending, break up the order of the notes, move them around to different positions and eventually transpose them to other keys. Remember to develop your lines by singing them. After the first part, there's a break in the rhythm section to give the soloist a chance to go it alone. Stay conscious of your timing here so you don't lose the groove.

C scale with ♭3 & ♭7

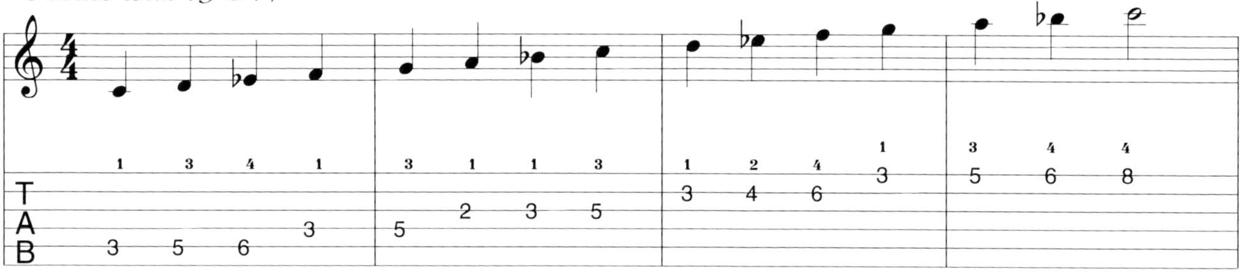

C minor pentatonic scale

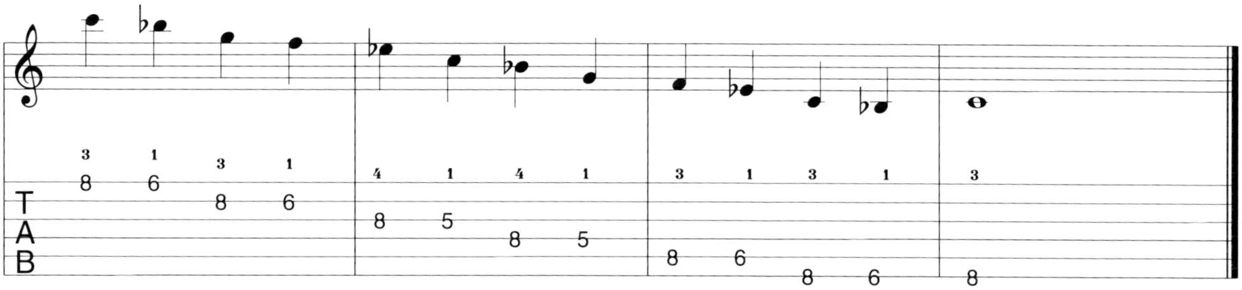

After you've mastered the melody, try the backup riff as written. Practice by playing along with the part on the CD. (You can isolate it by adjusting the balance on your stereo all the way to one side.) Eventually try integrating it into the melody to create a new solo. Use elements of both to create your own solo. You can use this type of funky backup in rock, R & B, blues, even country settings. Once you're comfortable playing it as written, vary it by turning around the lead-in notes like those in the pickup measure or measure two. Note the C chord voicing I used throughout the backup:

C

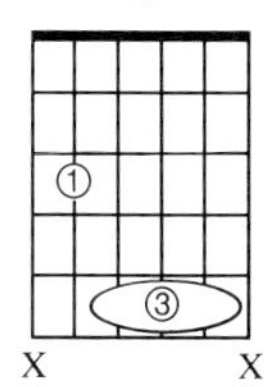

16 measure verse, chorus form. Five choruses. Key of C

Kissin' Ain't No Crime

by Dix Bruce

Kissin' Ain't No Crime

by Dix Bruce

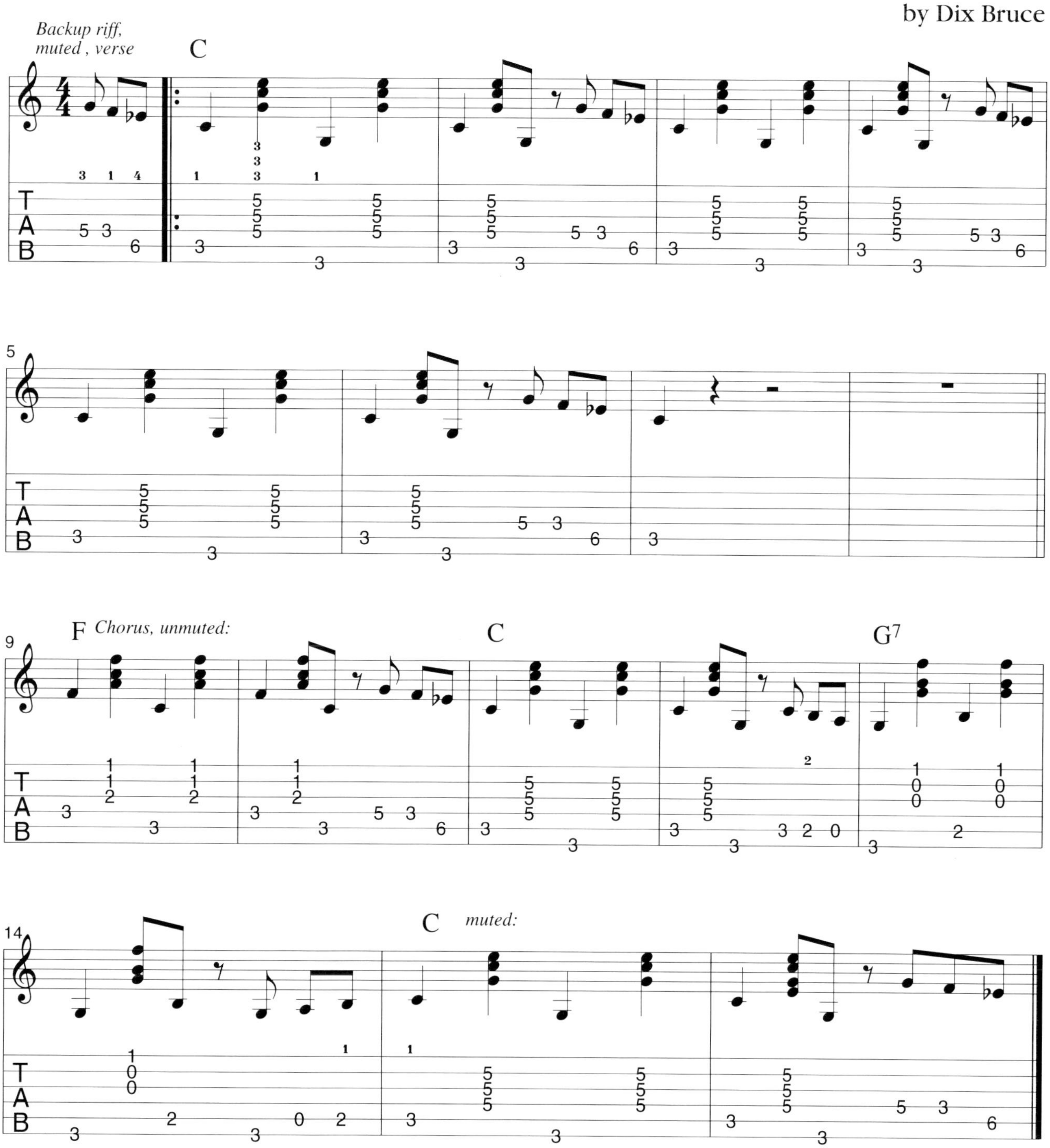

T-Model Ford Blues

Time to get loud! Here's our first tune with electric guitar, but of course you don't have to play it on electric. It's a riff blues in a Robben Ford style-modern urban-blues-rock vein. This type of tune, with its moving and chugging feel, is usually referred to as a shuffle. The form begins with a V, IV, I, V turnaround (the last four bars of the tune) and we'll repeat it as the ending to the tune.

The melody begins with a simple four measure riff (first four measures after the intro) which repeats over the IV7 chord (C7). The form ends with a new riff over the V7 chord (D7).

The changes on this blues are a little more involved than those we've had so far. Here, one measure of the I (G) is followed immediately with a measure of the IV7 (C7), then back to the I for a measure and then a measure of I7 (G7).

As on the other twelve bar riff blues, you can compose solos by simply making up two new riffs. Play the first riff over the first four bars, repeat it on the second four bars. Play your second riff over the last four bars and voila! you've got it! Of course, each riff has to fit over the specific chords in each part. The variations demonstrate these ideas and will give you two new solos, more if you mix and match the riffs. The first two riffs work over the first four bars and repeat on the second four bars. On the variation to "Memphis Minnie Blues" you moved the riff up an interval of a fourth to play over the IV chord. You can also do that here and create even more solos. The third and fourth variations work over the final four bars.

Be sure to make up as many of your own riffs as you can. Write them down in your spiral bound music notebook for easy reference. Index them by tune or by key. As you begin to feel more comfortable with making up and playing riffs, try plugging them into different songs in different keys on the CD. You will have to transpose them to the appropriate chords and keys.

Look again at "T-Model" variations. Analyze them and memorize the fretting hand positions they use. Understanding these positions and being able to adapt them to different tunes and keys can be incredibly helpful in understanding the guitar and blues on the guitar. The closed positions—those with no open notes—and their riffs, can be moved up and down on the fingerboard fairly easily if you maintain the relative finger/note positions.

"T-Model Ford Blues" uses the **V** chord in the key of G (D7) as a turnaround at the end of the form (M 16). On the last time through, take the second ending with its very brief **V** to end on the **I** chord (G).

(By the way that's me playing the bass on this one.)

12 measure form. Intro, seven choruses, turnaround ending. Key of G

T-Model Ford Blues

Intro turnaround:

by Dix Bruce

T-Model Ford Blues variations

by Dix Bruce

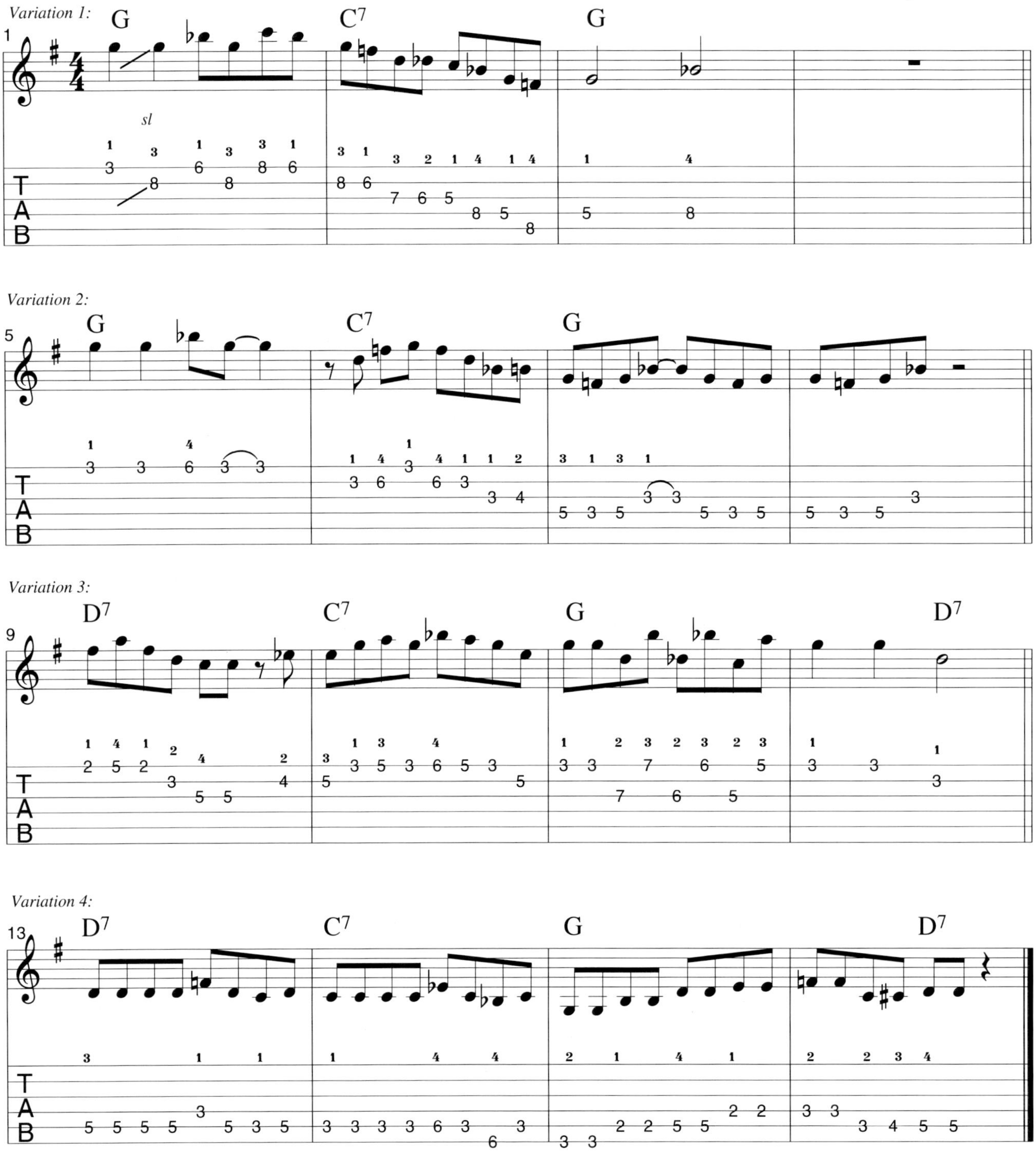

C MINOR BLUES

C Minor Blues is our first tune in a minor tonality. It was inspired by B.B. King's "The Thrill is Gone," and the introduction is a vamp on the Cm chord. The tune is presented in two keys, first in Cm, and then it modulates to Fm to give you practice transposing from one key to another.

The melody is pitched quite high and is played way up in the stratosphere, fret-wise. (I wanted to give you electric players some exercise.) Those of you playing acoustic, non-cutaway guitars should try it as written but may want to move it down an octave.

Try the minor pentatonic scales shown. The Cm pentatonic scale can be moved up five frets to make the Fm pentatonic scale. I've given the first few notes, you complete the rest. Use the same fingerings, simply transfer them, with their relative note positions in tact, up the neck. Likewise, the first Fm pentatonic scale can be moved up to make a Cm pentatonic. Simply begin the same scale with the first finger on the eighth fret, sixth string. Practice playing these closed position, moveable pentatonic scales all over the neck so that you can play them both over any minor chord. Then try them over their corresponding *major* chords. Do you like the sound?

C minor pentatonic scale

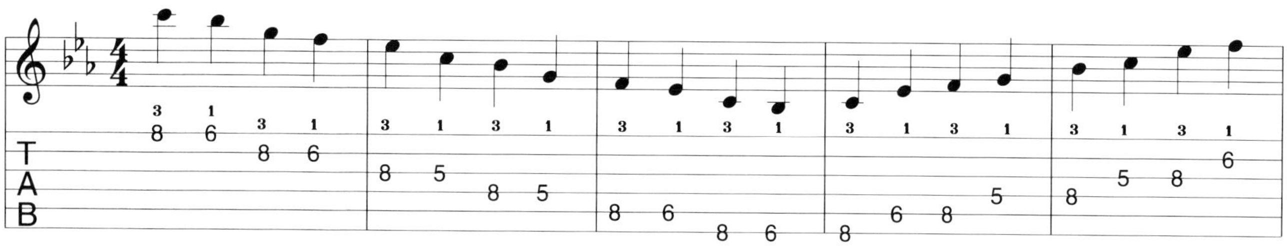

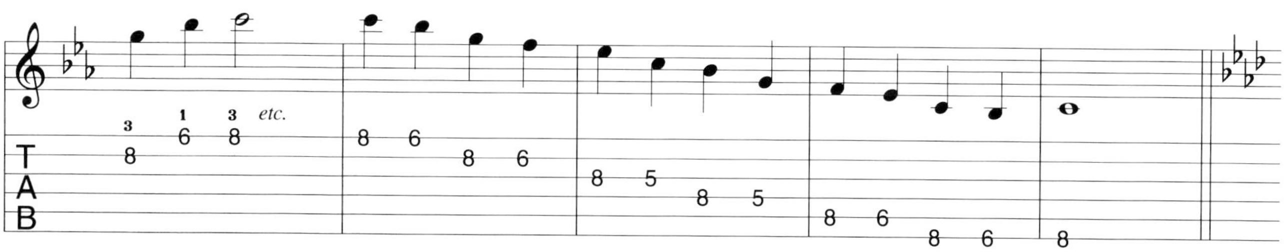

F minor pentatonic scale

F minor pentatonic scale, upper octave

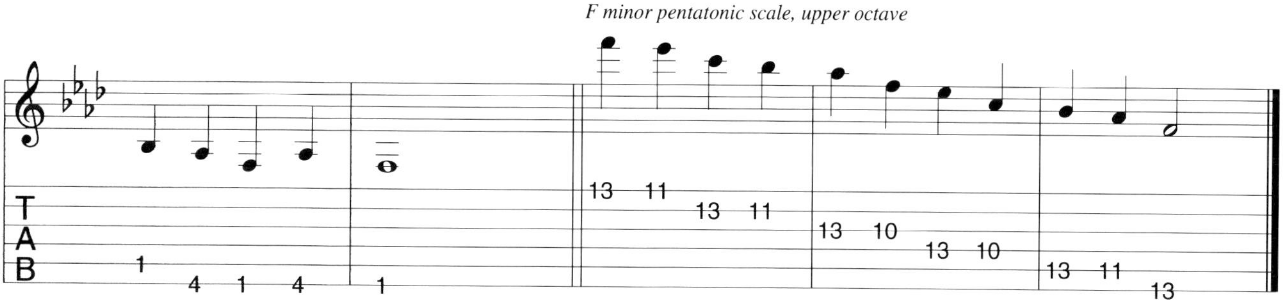

C MINOR BLUES

On the ♯V–V change (A♭7–G7 or D♭7–C7), try playing arpeggios made up of only the tones of the chords.

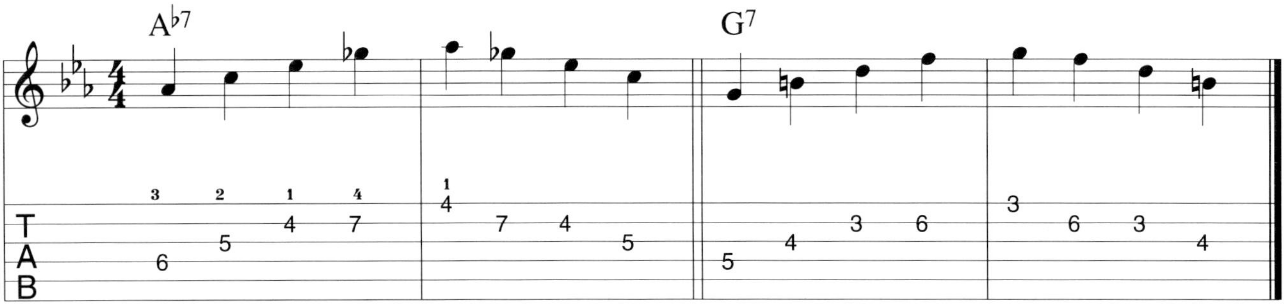

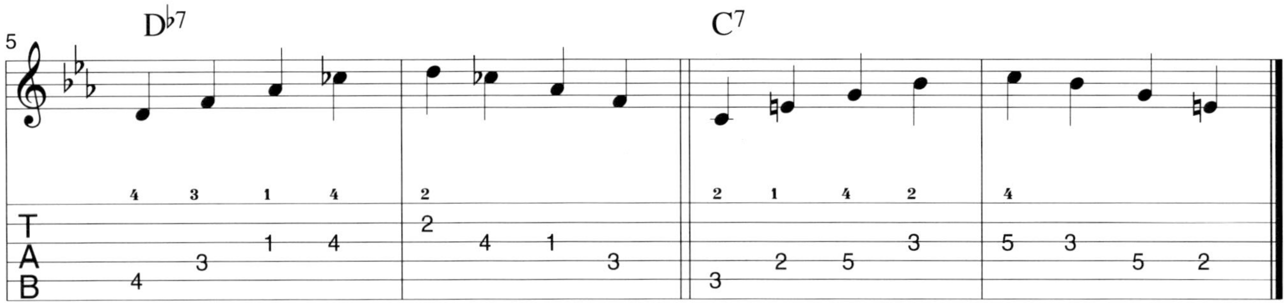

Below you'll find a few riffs to try out on the changes shown. On variations five and six, you'll have to add two measures of Cm to resolve the melodic phrase. Make up your own or use the first two measures of the song.

We're getting to the point where we've learned quite a few riffs, scales, and now even some chord tones and arpeggios. They're all building blocks toward expressing yourself musically, like words are the building blocks of speech. The trick is to combine them in a meaningful way and avoid tossing them around randomly. (Ever heard Sylvester Stallone talk about "…bewailing that particular epistemology…"?) One way you can avoid this "worthless foam from the mouth" (*) or in this case the fingers (not a pleasant image either way I know, but stay with me) is to sing what you intend to play before you play it. (I know I keep pestering you about this, but, doggone it, it's important! You're trying to train yourself to make that guitar sing, and to sing melodies. You want those melodies to be from your heart, your experience, not just meaningless scalar junk. Someday you'll thank me, probably from the stage of the Grammy Award show. So there!) Put it together in your head before you let it escape through your fingers. It's a difficult habit to establish, but once you can do it, your chances of playing dribble are much reduced. And, in the process, you'll train your heart, head, and hands to work together musically.

12 measure form. Four measure vamp at beginning, four choruses in Cm then modulation to Fm and two more choruses. Repeat the last four measures for turnaround at end. Key of C minor and F minor.

* (Be the first to write and tell me who used that term in what song and I'll send you one of my recordings! Send your answer to Musix, PO Box 231005, Pleasant Hill, CA 94523.)

C minor Blues variations

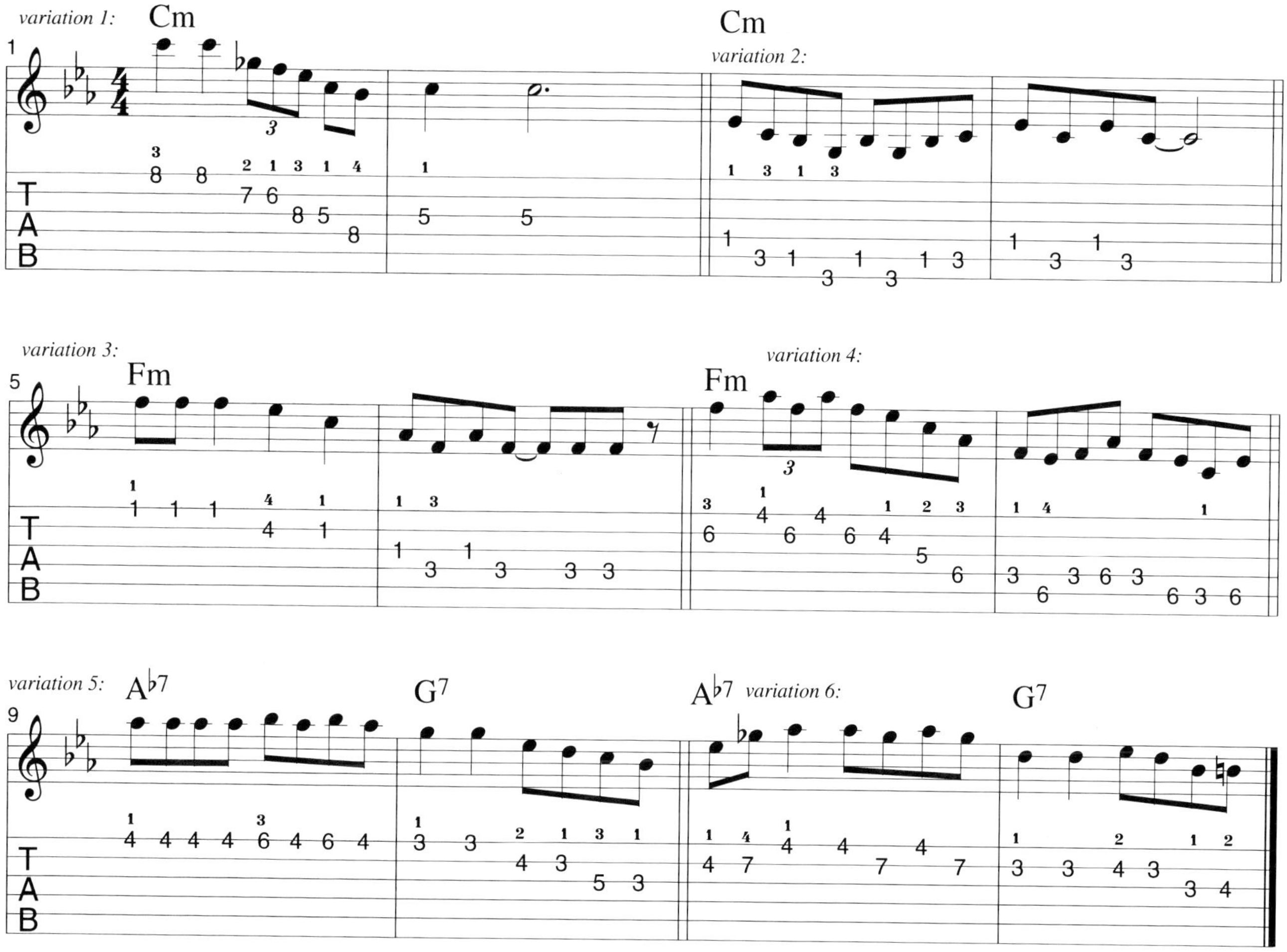

Resolve both licks to a Cm chord.

C minor Blues

by Dix Bruce

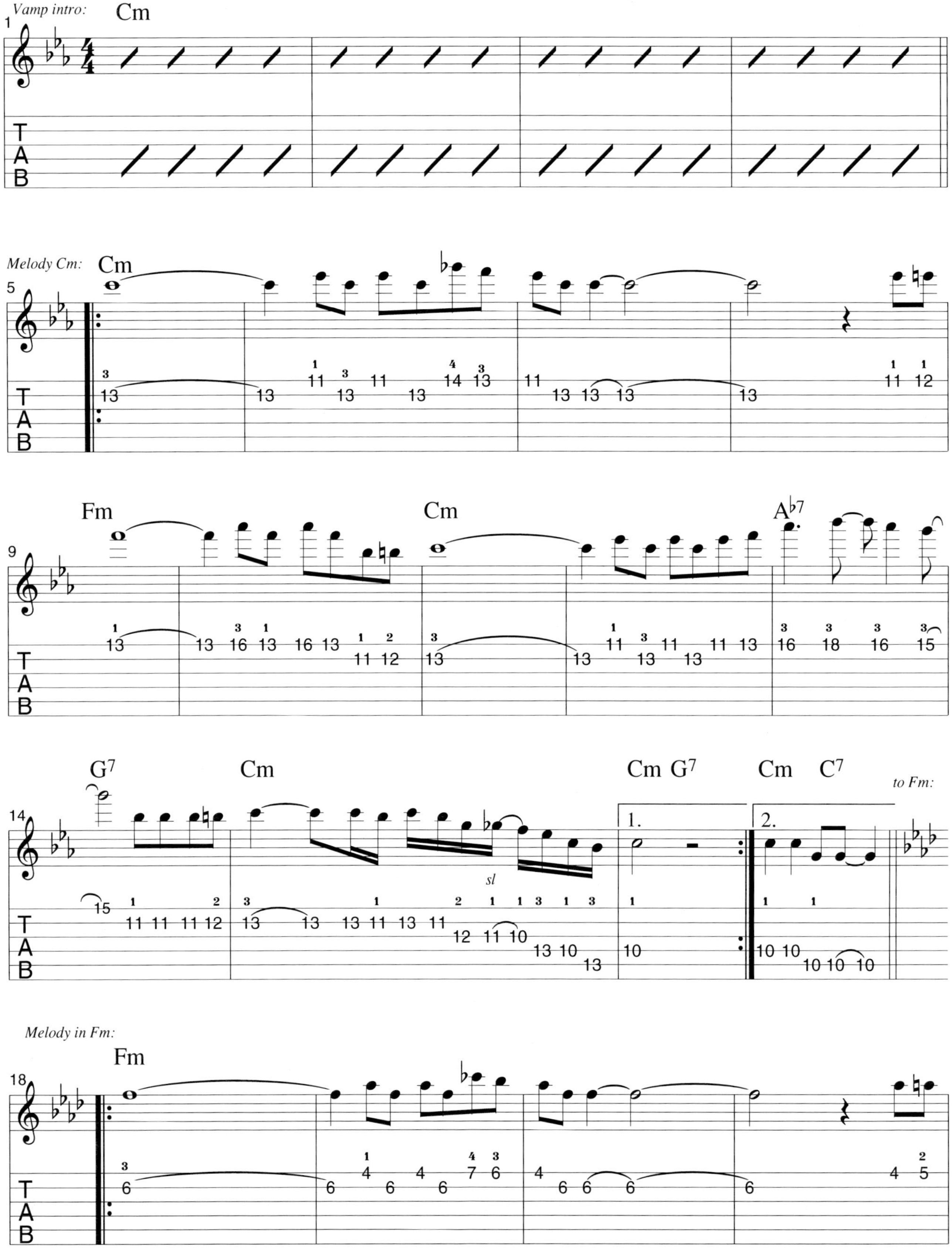

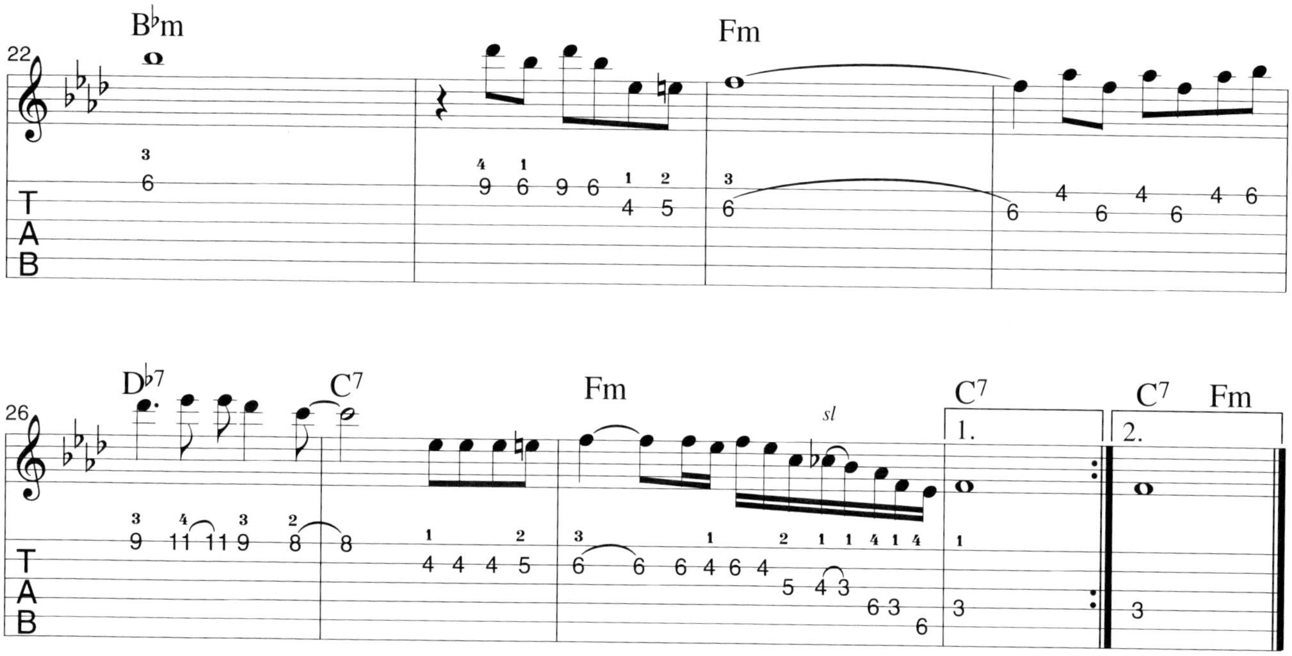
B♭m
Fm
D♭7
C7
Fm
sl
C7
1.
C7
2.
Fm

Honey Babe

Honey Babe has one of my favorite grooves: kind of an easy going and laid back Eric Clapton "Lay Down Sally" thing. Think of it as an "uptempo Texas/country blues." The form is a little unusual being only eight bars in length rather than the more common twelve or sixteen bars. A solo should be thought of as two times through the progression. Think of this as a sixteen bar form. Flatpickers can leave out all the bass notes (generally strings 6, 5, and 4) normally played with the thumb.

The variation is built around very prominent flat seven and flat third sounds: third fret second string D for the flat seventh of the E chord; third fret first string G natural for the flat third of the E chord, etc.

Sixteen measure form. Six choruses. Key of E.

by Dix Bruce

The Highway Blues

The Highway Blues, a "slow shuffle," has a couple different chord moves. The introduction, as well as the last four bars of the form, is played over a I-VI-II-V ("one-six-two-five") chord progression with mostly dominant seven chords. I-VI-II-Vs, in this case F-D7-G7-C7, are quite prevalent in jazz and pop music but you'll also find them in a lot of blues, especially blues tinged with jazz or ragtime. Another chordal difference is the movement from the I (F) chord in the first measure to the V (C7) in the second. Up to this point, most of the tunes have used the more common chordal movement of I to IV.

Note that there is a **V** chord (C7) turnaround in the last measure. Play it when you repeat to the top of the form. On the last time through, leave it out and only play the **I** (F).

The variations are licks you can use on any I-VI-II-V progression that has dominant seven chords like these. You will also run into progressions without the dominant seven chords, e.g. I-vi-ii-V or F-Dm-Gm-C7, and these dominant seven licks will have to be modified to fit. The trick is to determine whether the second and third chords are dominant or minor as both progressions are referred to as "one-six-two-five." Once you learn these variations, plug them in to "The Highway Blues" as substitutes for what is written and also transpose them to other keys and tunes. And, of course, don't forget to make up your own.

Incidentally, measures eleven and twelve should sound very familiar to you. I'm sure you've heard them before. They make up a little ending tag that's used *everywhere* in all types of blues. It's a cool little lick that you should learn to play in every key. It's sure to come in handy.

Sixteen measure form. Four measure introduction. Three choruses. Key of F.

The Highway Blues

by Dix Bruce

Jump Blues

Jump Blues is an example of a late 40s, early 50s, "fast rhythm & blues" feel. The key of A♭ may be a little difficult for you at first, but once you get used to it, it's just another key, and it's important that you be able to play in any key. Flat keys like B♭, E♭, etc., will be especially useful if you like jump blues and R & B, since those forms are reed and brass driven and horn guys rarely play in the sharp keys guitarists like.

Again, "Jump Blues" is a simple riff blues: the first four bars are repeated to make the second four bars. The variations offer a couple different riffs you can plug into the first eight bars of the progression. You'll have to come up with the last four bars on your own! *Just a reminder:* Play the turnaround V chord in M 12 on the repeats, leave it out the last time through.

Twelve measure form. Ten choruses. Key of A♭.

by Dix Bruce

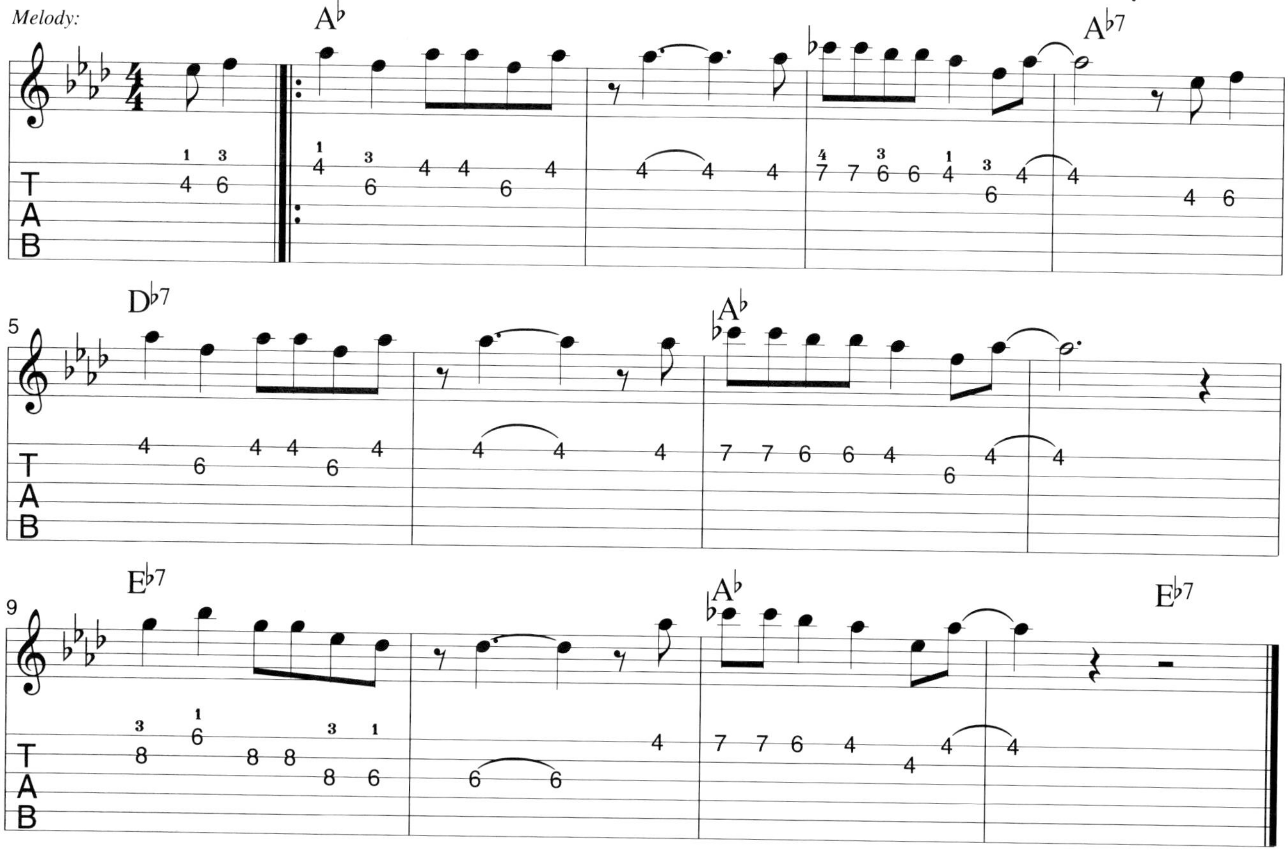

Frogs For Snakes

Frogs For Snakes is a low down "delta/Texas-style" blues with a triplet-based melody. You've probably heard the opening lick a thousand times. Make sure you play both notes of the double stops (when you play two notes at once) throughout the melody. In measure five you'll need to use the alternate A chord shown at right, which I have heard referred to as the "hoe handle A." Unlike most of the previous tunes, I added a ♯V ("sharp five") chord (C7) in the tenth measure for variation. Make sure that you don't skip over it in your solos! If you're not fingerpicking, you can leave out the bass notes all together and play the melody with a pick.

A*

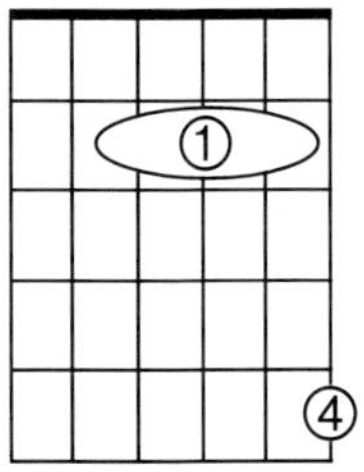

The variation, while rooted on the theme of the melody, demonstrates how you carry one basic lick through the first eight bars of chord changes.

(P.S.- End the tune on the E chord, not the B7.)

12 measure form. Four choruses. Key of E.

by Dix Bruce

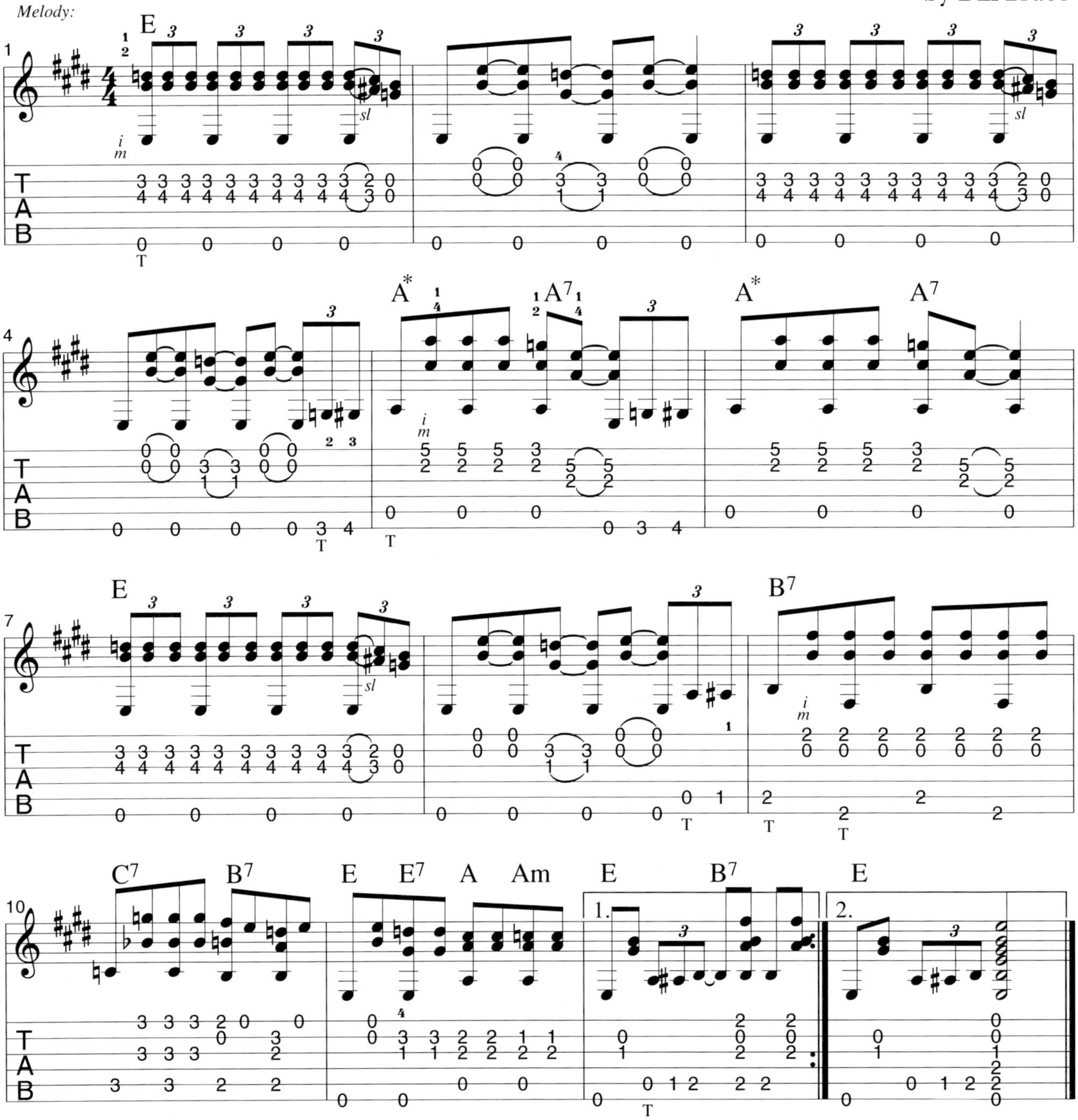

Frogs For Snakes

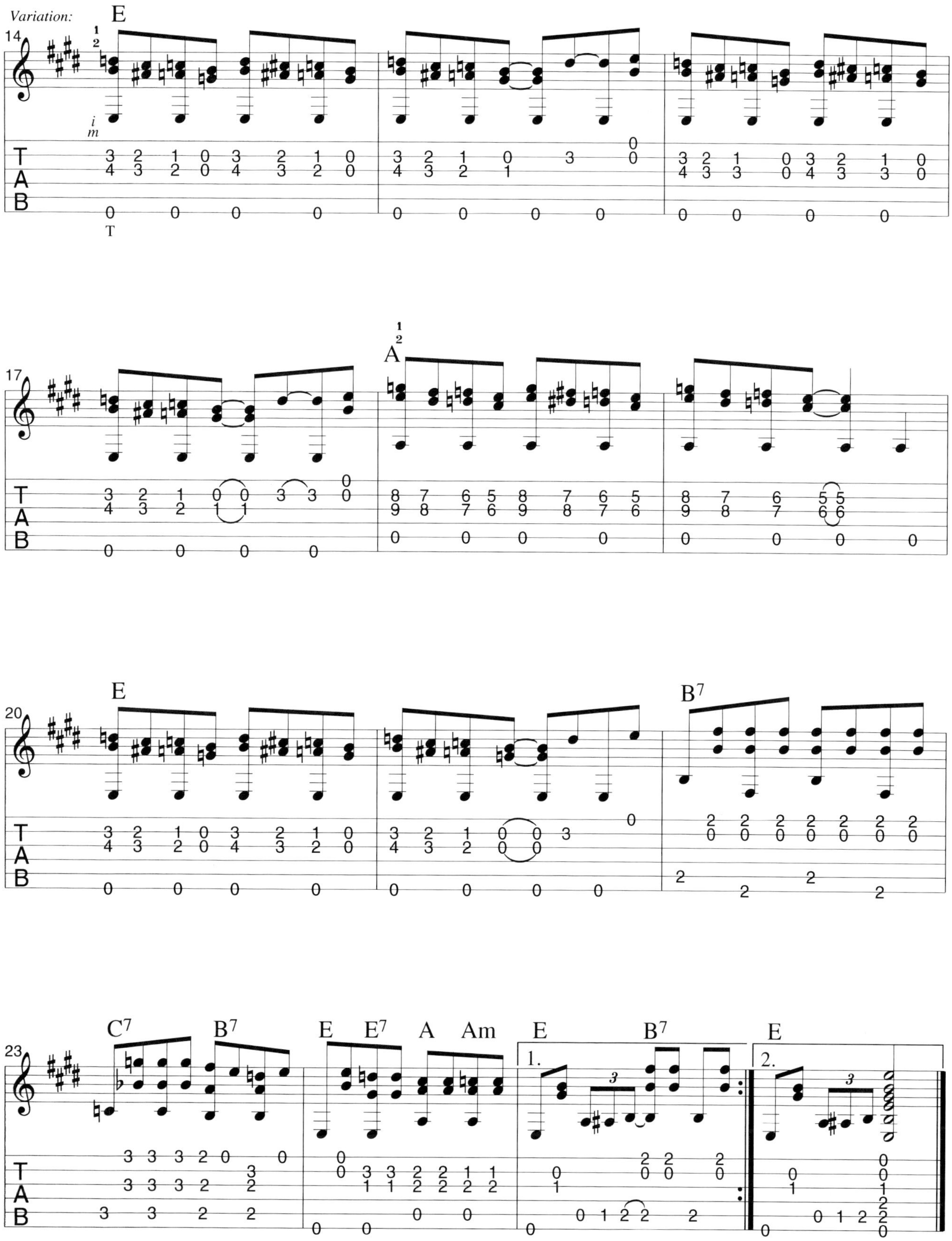

G minor Blues

A medium "tempo, modern/urban blues," this time in Gm. I got the hard, stinging, sound on the recording of the melody by picking with my index finger, pulling up on the strings and letting them slap back onto the fingerboard. Four two measure variations are given: two for the G minor chord and two for the D7. Transpose the Gm licks up two and one half steps (five frets) and use them on the Cm. As you did on "The C Minor Blues," resolve the D7 licks by adding two of your own measures of Gm licks.

12 measure form. Five choruses. Key of G minor.

by Dix Bruce

Tuxedo Blues

Here's another type of groove for you, kind of a "rock & roll rhumba" with an early 1960s feel and a melody with double stops. I play the lower notes with a flatpick between my thumb and first finger and fingerpick the upper notes with my second finger. If you want to play just one of the parts, I suggest the upper, which you can flatpick or fingerpick. Invite a friend to play the other part.

I used the D7+ (D7 augmented fifth) (see chord diagram below) in the beginning and also at the end of the melody to give the progression that extra pull back to the I (G) chord. To make an augmented chord, we raise the fifth of the chord one half step. In this case we raise the A note up an A♯. This makes for quite an unstable interval and your ear wants to take it somewhere more settled, either up or down! In the same chord you also have the flat seven of the V chord (a C note on a D chord) which makes another unstable interval and your ear wants *it* to go down to B or up to D. We resolve it all by moving to that nice, stable, restful G chord!

For variations, try plugging in melody or variation licks from the other tunes in this book and be sure to make up your own. Fitting licks you know into a new situation is invaluable as practice for your musical vocabulary and one of the most useful exercises you can work through.

"Tuxedo Blues" is also included on my "Tuxedo Blues" recording. *(See page 4.)*

Sixteen measure form. Six choruses. Key of G.

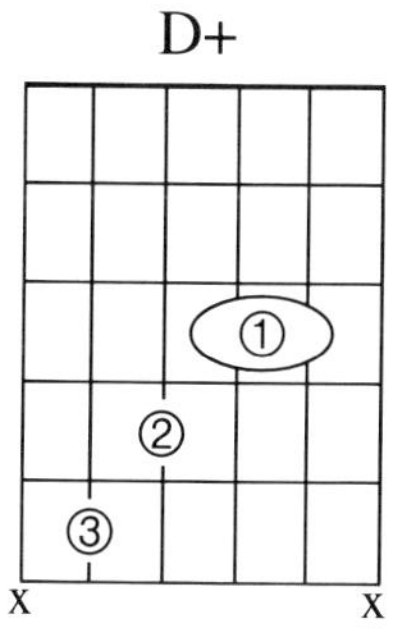

Tuxedo Blues

by Dix Bruce

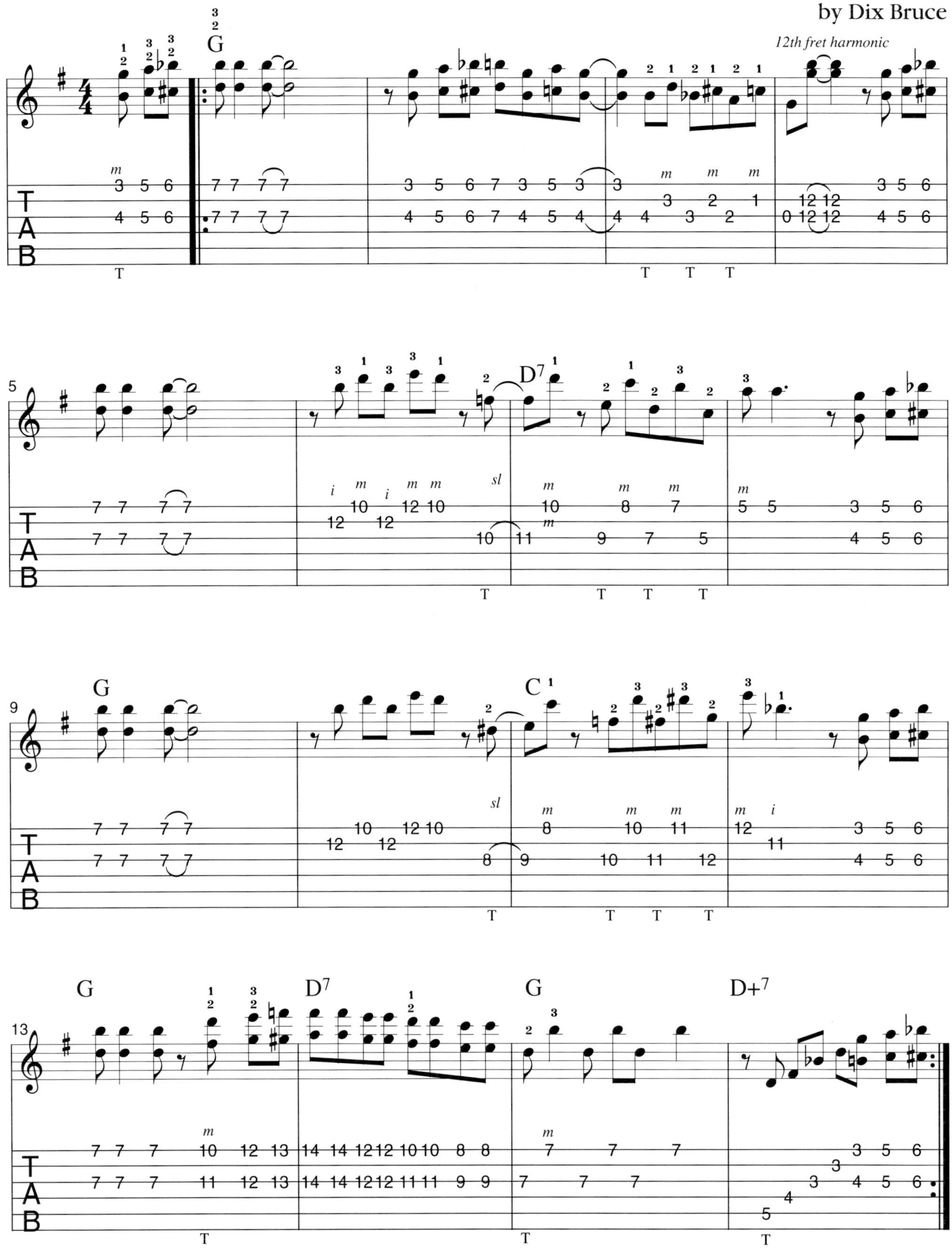

Rockabilly Boogie

Rockabilly Boogie is a simple boogie woogie set to a rockabilly groove. The only unusual thing about it is the F♯m7 (a ii m7 or "two minor seven") chord I added in the ninth measure.

Bend the first three notes, G naturals stretched up to G♯, with the third finger of your fretting hand. While you can use this technique on any guitar, I especially like the twang I got on my Telecaster. The first two variations are typical boogie woogie riffs where I inverted the motion of the melodic line. The first of them, which uses quarter notes, is a bit easier than the second eighth note example. You'll use the same basic fingerings and hand positions you used in the melody. Following these are a couple of riffs which work over the ii-V (F♯m7-B7) changes. Remember: make up your own. Write them down in a bound music notebook so you don't loose track of every brilliant lick!

Twelve measure form. Twelve choruses. Key of E.

Rockabilly Boogie

by Dix Bruce

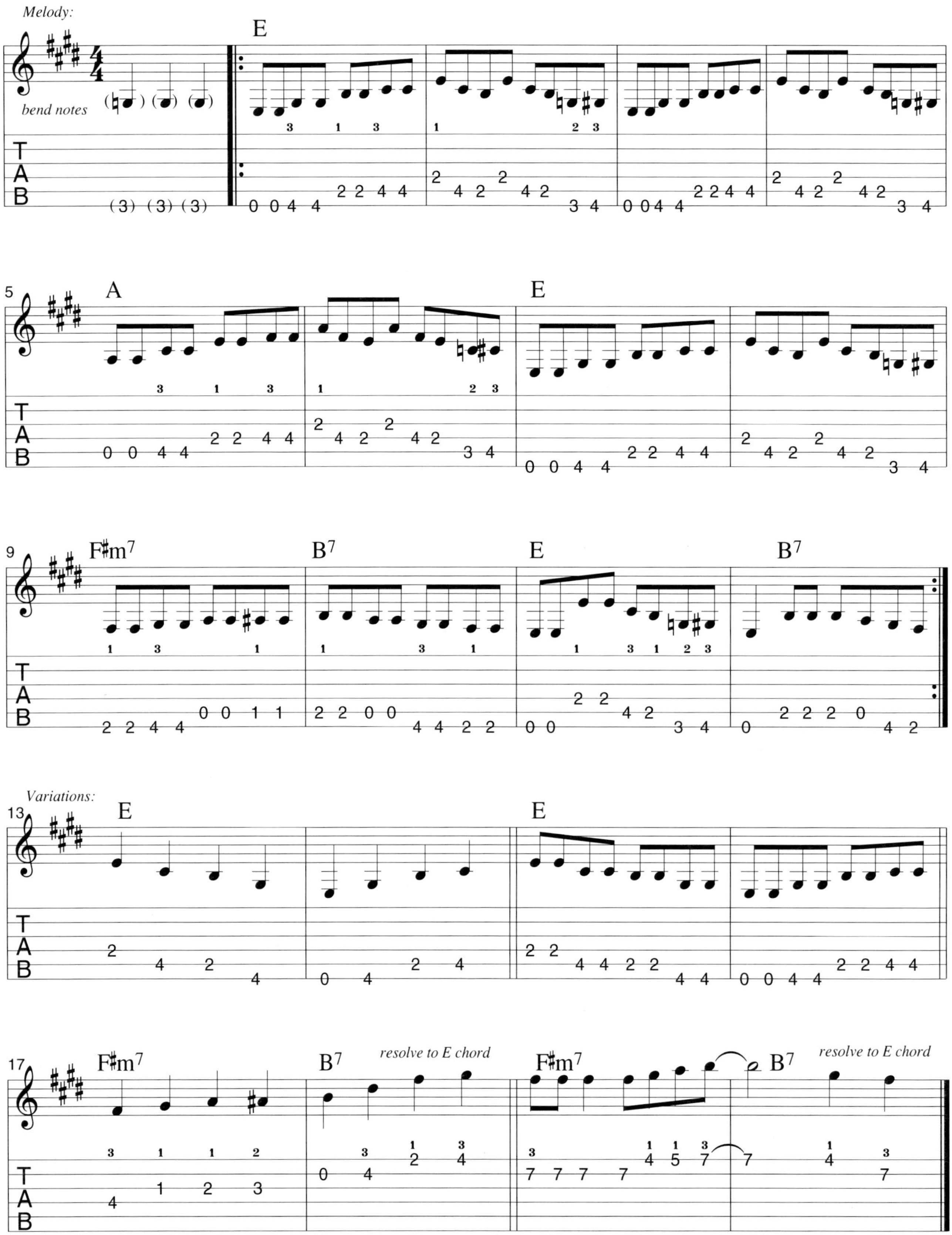

Cream in My Coffee

Cream in My Coffee is probably the most challenging tune of the set. I think of it as a "jazz blues" with its longer form and more involved chord progression. I've identified the three different parts of the song as "A," "B," and "C." "A" is sixteen bars in length, the "B" part (or bridge) is eight bars long, "C" is also eight bars long and has the same chord progression as the second eight bars of "A."

The "up-the-neck" positions will give all your fingers quite a workout. Again, I tried to keep the fretting finger notations to a minimum by not repeating a finger/fret number that's just been used or is obvious from the basic hand position you're using.

In the fourth chorus you'll hear breaks for a bass solo. Concentrate on staying with the groove without speeding up or slowing down. Repeat the last four bars as an ending on the fourth chorus.

The variation can be plugged into the bridge or "B" part.

A version of "Cream in My Coffee" is included on my "Tuxedo Blues" recording. *(See page 4.)*

Thirty two measure form. Four choruses plus ending. Key of B♭.

Variation:

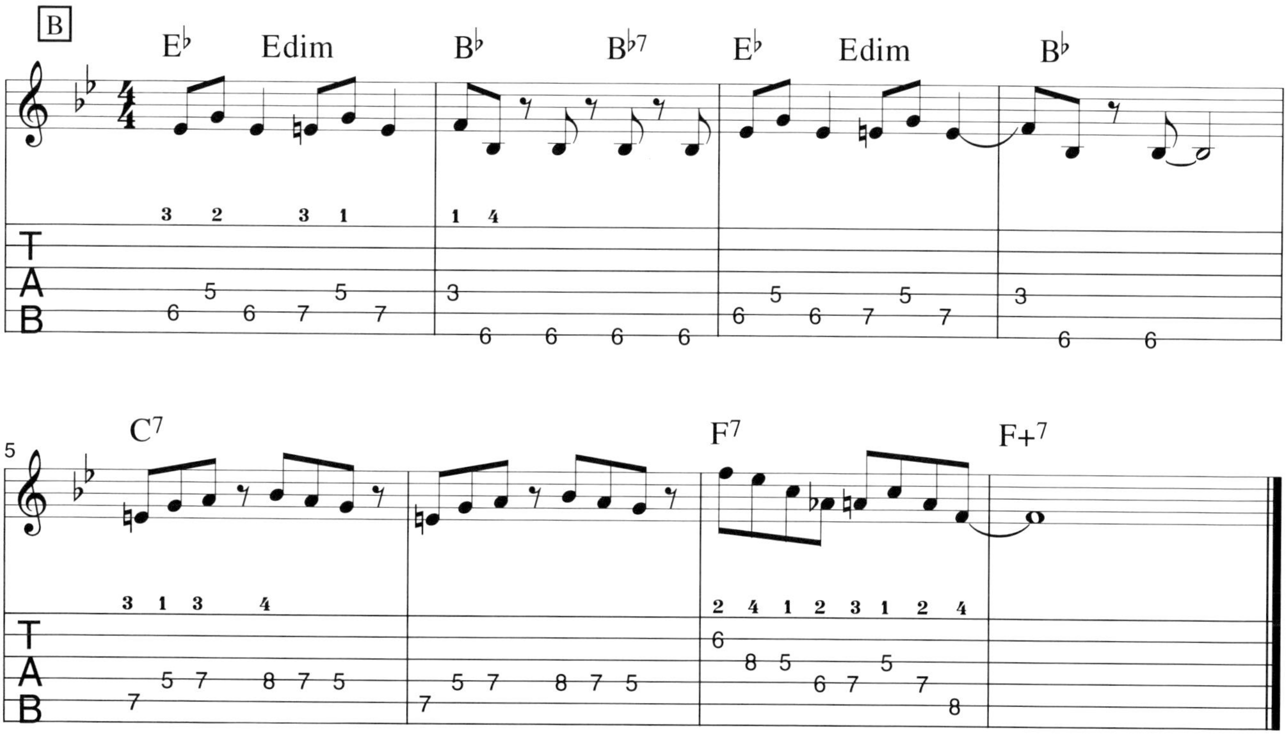

Cream in My Coffee

by Dix Bruce

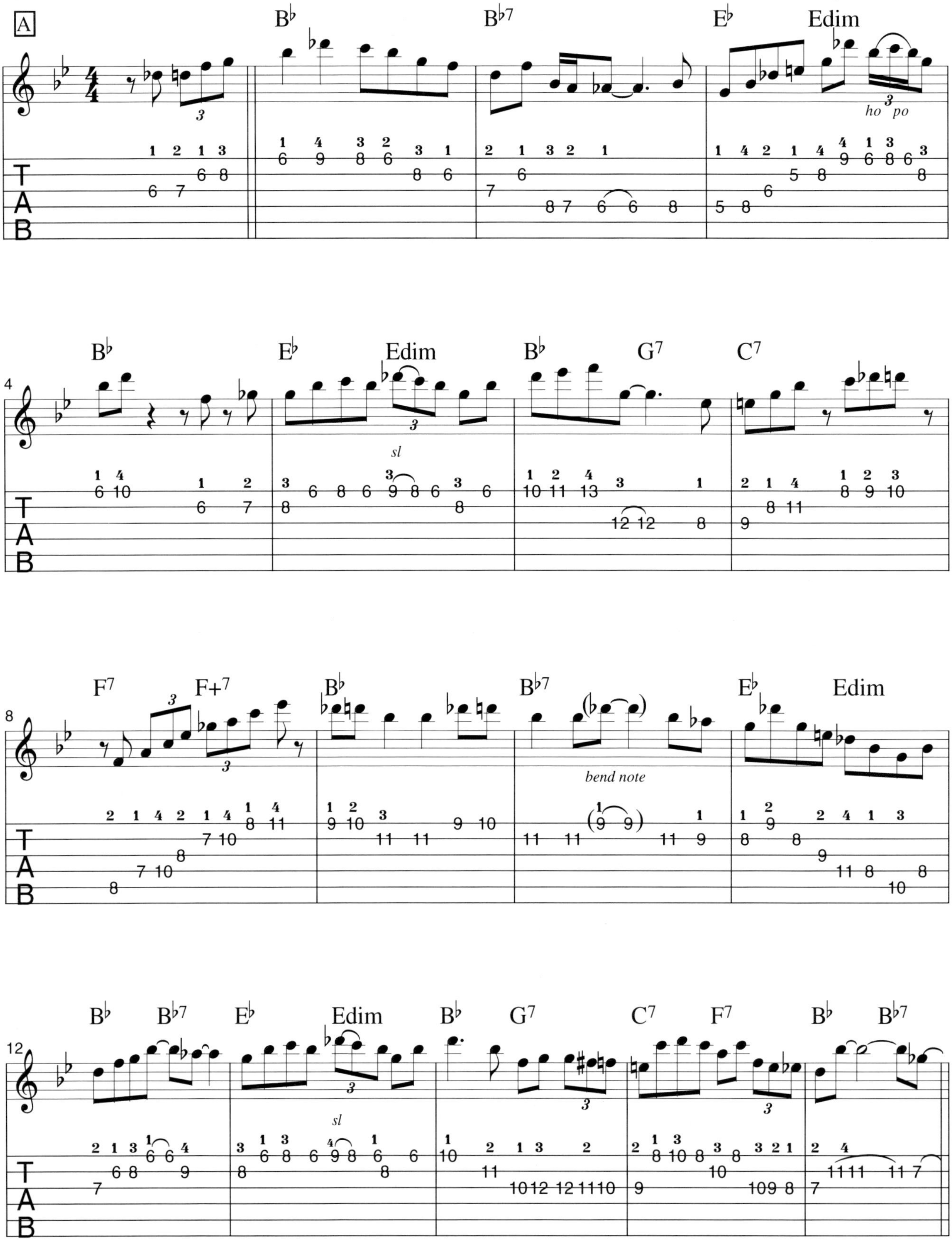

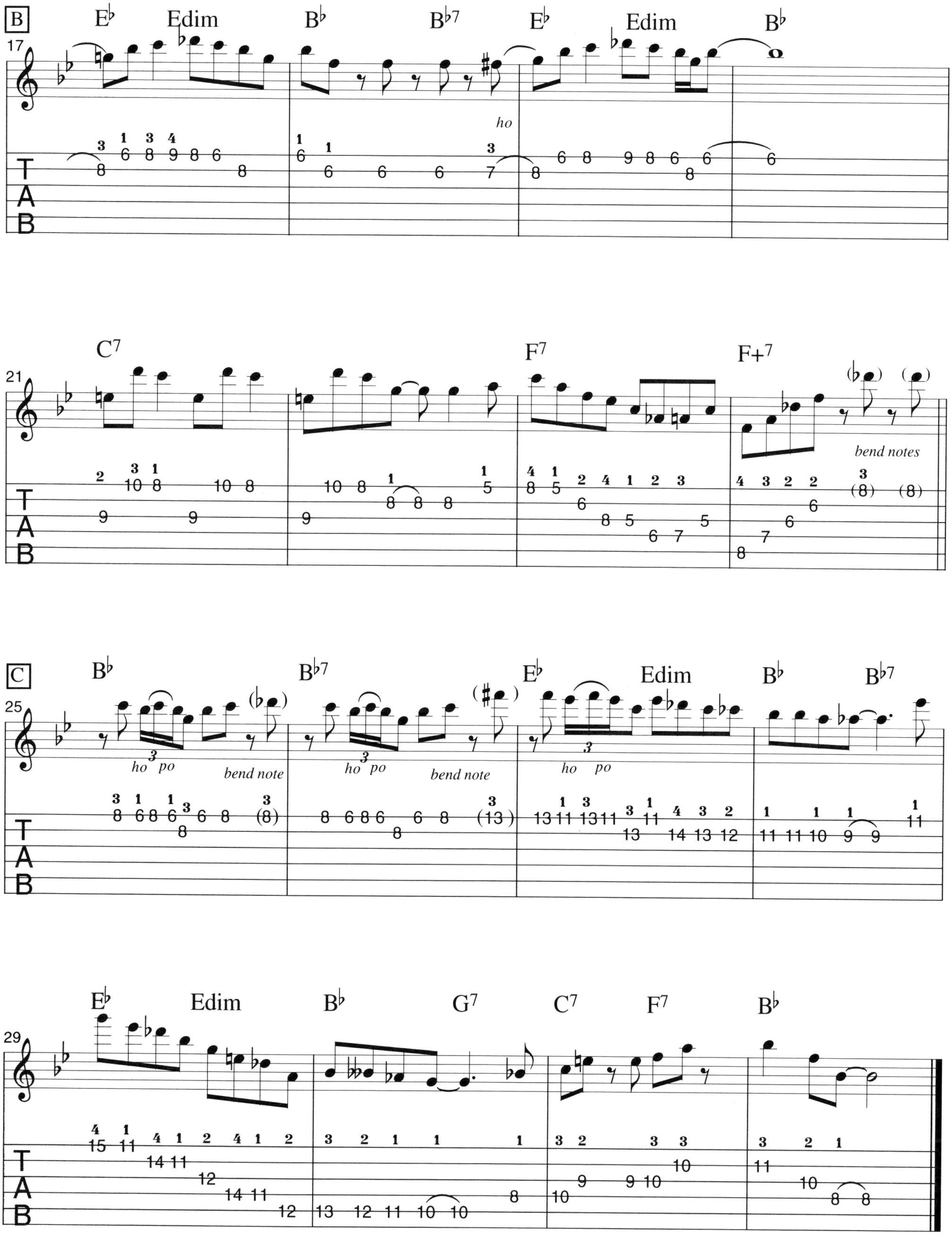
B
E♭ Edim B♭ B♭7 E♭ Edim B♭
ho
TAB
C7 F7 F+7
bend notes
TAB
C
B♭ B♭7 E♭ Edim B♭ B♭7
ho po bend note
ho po bend note
ho po
TAB
E♭ Edim B♭ G7 C7 F7 B♭
TAB

Afterword

Congratulations! You've made it through! Take a deep breath, give yourself a pat on the back, and shake your own hand. That done it's now time to go back and play through the tunes again! (Just kidding, rest a minute.)

Playing is the most important thing you can do to learn and improve. I know that seems obvious but I mention it here because of the large number of students I've met who think of music as an intellectual exercise. Wrong! You've gotta get in there and blow or pick or pound—you can't just read about it.

Listening is equally important. Recordings are the most accessible source for this music, but don't ignore the power of hearing the music live. Seek out local blues musicians and get to know them. Learn their tunes and find opportunities to jam with them. Analyze their approach to the music and ask about their sources. *(See the list of guitarists on page 48.)*

Be sure to write me with your comments, questions and banjo jokes c/o MUSIX, PO Box 231005, Pleasant Hill, CA 94523. Our e-mail is: dix@musixnow.com

Have fun!

The Band

photo by Rob Thomas

Dix Bruce, guitar

photo by Dix Bruce

Chris Sandoval, drums

photo by Dix Bruce

Steve Hanson, bass

photo by Dix Bruce

Bruce Gordon, keyboards

photo by Kari Waitzfelder

Rick Hatfield, harmonica

BackUP TRAX: Basic Blues Guitar Chords

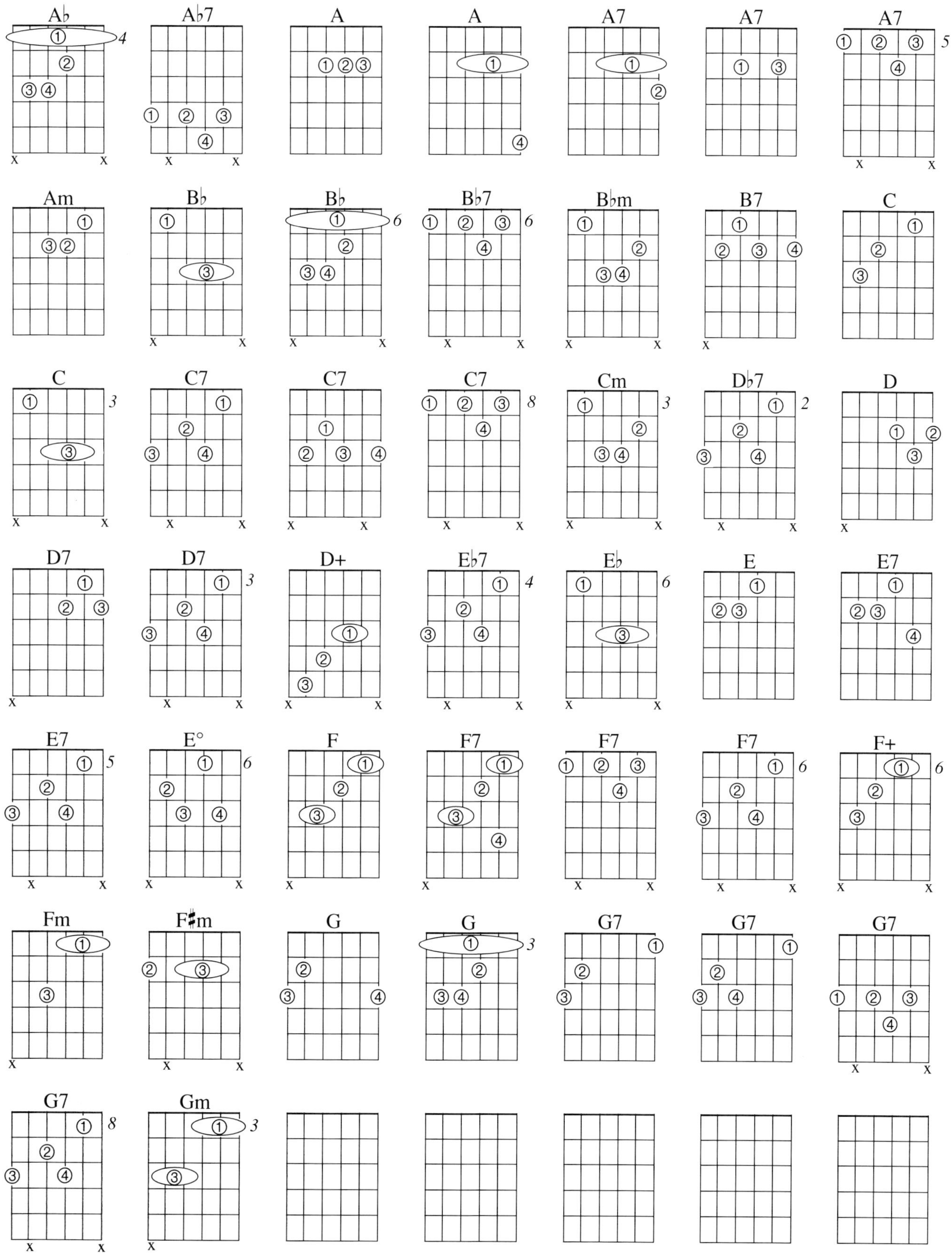

Blues Guitarists

As I mentioned before, it's important that you explore the ways that other guitarists approach the blues. Below is a listing of some artists you might enjoy. Sorry if I've left out your favorites. My aim was to include a range of styles similar to those covered in this book. Most large record stores should have these artists in stock. As you explore the blues, make sure that you listen to other instrumentalists and singers, not just guitar players. You'll find that your most interesting ideas can come from pianists, sax players, harmonicats, etc. Listen for sounds that you can adapt to make part of your vocabulary!

Luther Allison
Etta Baker
Blind Blake
Rory Block
Michael Bloomfield
Barbecue Bob
Juke Boy Bonner
Big Bill Broonzy
Clarence "Gatemouth" Brown
Bo Carter
Eric Clapton
Albert Collins
Elizabeth Cotten
Robert Cray
Arthur "Big Boy" Crudup
Rev. Gary Davis
Jimmy Dawkins
Snooks Eaglin
Sleepy John Estes
Sue Foley
Robben Ford
Blind Boy Fuller
Jesse Fuller
Lowell Fulson
Buddy Guy
John Hammond
Slim Harpo
Alvin Youngblood Hart
Earl Hooker
John Lee Hooker
Lightning Hopkins
Son House

Mississippi John Hurt
J.B. Hutto
Lil Son Jackson
Elmore James
Skip James
Blind Lemon Jefferson
Lonnie Johnson
Robert Johnson
Albert King
B.B. King
Freddie King
Leadbelly
Mance Lipscomb
Fred McDowell
Brownie McGee
Blind Willie McTell
Memphis Minnie
Charley Patton
Ann Rabson
Tampa Red
Jimmy Reed
Otis Rush
Hound Dog Taylor
Stevie Ray Vaughan
T-Bone Walker
Muddy Waters
Bukka White
Josh White
Big Joe Williams
Howlin' Wolf
Johnny Young
Your Name Here